The information contained in this book is based on the author's research and experience. While the author has made every effort to provide accurate and up-to-date information, errors and omissions may occur. The author and publisher assume no responsibility for any errors or omissions or for any actions taken based on the information contained in this book.

The information contained in this book is provided "as is," without warranty of any kind, express or implied, including but not limited to the warranties of merchantability, fitness for a particular purpose, or non-infringement. In no event shall the author or publisher be liable for any claim, damages, or other liability, whether in an action of contract, tort, or otherwise, arising from, out of, or in connection with the book or the use or other dealings in the book.

1

TABLE OF CONTENTS

INTRODUCTION

In today's digital realm, where information inundates every corner of our online existence, capturing and retaining the attention of potential customers has become both an art and a science. Enter content marketing – the strategic linchpin that businesses, irrespective of size or industry, are leveraging to navigate this landscape and forge meaningful connections with their audiences.

Content marketing is more than a mere promotional tool; it's an encompassing approach that revolves around creating, distributing, and amplifying valuable, relevant, and consistent content to attract, engage, and retain a specific target audience. Unlike traditional advertising, content marketing isn't solely fixated on sales pitches; instead, it aims to provide genuine value to consumers, nurturing trust and fostering long-term relationships.

In essence, content marketing is the heartbeat of modern business strategies. Its significance lies in its ability to cut through the digital noise, acting as a beacon that guides customers toward brands that resonate with their needs, preferences, and aspirations. Through compelling storytelling, informative blog posts, captivating videos, engaging social media content, podcasts, and more, content marketing enables businesses to establish themselves as authoritative voices within their niches.

Now, why is content marketing essential for businesses in today's landscape? The answer lies in the profound shift in consumer behavior. Today's consumers are discerning, empowered, and actively seek more than just products or services; they crave meaningful experiences, valuable information, and authenticity from the brands they interact with. Content marketing provides precisely that—a platform to engage authentically, educate, entertain, and build relationships based on mutual trust.

Moreover, the digital era has fundamentally transformed how consumers research, evaluate, and make purchasing decisions. Gone are the days of passive consumption; instead, consumers actively seek information, reviews, and insights before committing to a brand or making a purchase. Content marketing positions businesses as not just sellers but as reliable sources of information, aiding consumers in their decision-making process while subtly guiding them towards choosing their offerings.

Furthermore, content marketing isn't confined to a single marketing channel; it thrives across various platforms and mediums, adapting seamlessly to the diverse preferences of today's audiences. Whether it's through social media, search engines, email, podcasts, or visual storytelling, content marketing flexes its versatility, meeting consumers where they are and offering valuable content tailored to their tastes.

In this age where authenticity, relevance, and trust reign supreme, content marketing emerges as the cornerstone of successful business strategies. It's the catalyst that sparks conversations, builds communities, drives brand loyalty, and ultimately, fuels sustainable growth in an ever-evolving digital landscape. As we delve deeper into this guide, we'll uncover the intricacies, strategies, and insights needed to embark on a rewarding content marketing journey.

CHAPTER ONE

WHAT IS CONTENT MARKETING?

Content marketing is a strategic marketing approach focused on creating, publishing, and distributing valuable, relevant, and consistent content to attract, engage, and retain a clearly defined audience. Unlike traditional advertising, which directly promotes products or services, content marketing aims to provide informative, entertaining, or educational content that addresses the needs, interests, and pain points of the target audience.

The primary goal of content marketing is not just to sell but to build trust, establish credibility, and nurture long-term relationships with customers. It involves creating various types of content, such as blog posts, articles, videos, infographics, podcasts, social media posts, eBooks, webinars, and more, tailored to resonate with the specific interests and preferences of the intended audience.

Effective content marketing doesn't interrupt or intrude on the audience's online experience but rather seeks to add value by offering relevant information, entertainment, or solutions to their problems. By consistently delivering valuable content, businesses aim to attract and retain a loyal audience, ultimately driving profitable customer action, whether it's making a purchase, subscribing to a service, or sharing content with others.

Content marketing operates on the principle of reciprocity, providing something of value to the audience before expecting anything in return. Over time, this approach can position a brand as an authority or thought leader in its industry, resulting in increased brand awareness, improved customer loyalty, and ultimately, business growth.

In essence, content marketing is about building relationships, fostering engagement, and delivering meaningful content that resonates with the target audience, all while aligning with the broader marketing goals and objectives of a business or organization.

SIGNIFICANCE OF CONTENT MARKETING IN TODAY'S DIGITAL LANDSCAPE

Content marketing holds significant importance in today's digital landscape due to several key reasons:

• Audience Engagement and Trust: In an era where consumers have become more discerning, content marketing offers a way to engage audiences authentically. By providing valuable, relevant, and insightful content, businesses can build trust, credibility, and a loyal following.

• Visibility and Brand Awareness: With the immense volume of online content available, businesses need to stand out. Content marketing helps in increasing brand visibility by creating quality content that attracts and retains attention, making the brand more recognizable among competitors.

• Relationship Building and Customer Retention: Content marketing focuses on nurturing relationships rather than just making sales. It helps in retaining existing customers by continually providing them with valuable information, which, in turn, strengthens brand loyalty.

• SEO and Organic Traffic: Search engines favor fresh, high-quality content. Content marketing aids in SEO efforts by providing relevant material for search engines to index, thereby improving a website's ranking and attracting organic traffic.

• Educating and Informing Consumers: Modern consumers prefer making informed decisions. Content marketing provides a platform to educate and inform customers about products, services, industry trends, and solutions to their problems, empowering them to make better choices.

• Multi-Channel Reach: Through various content formats (blogs, videos, social media, podcasts, etc.), content marketing allows businesses to reach audiences across different platforms and devices, catering to diverse preferences and behaviors.

• Data Collection and Analysis: Content marketing generates data on audience behavior, preferences, and interactions. Analyzing this data helps in refining marketing strategies, understanding customer needs better, and creating more targeted and effective content.

• Cost-Effectiveness and Long-Term Results: Compared to traditional advertising, content marketing can be more cost-effective and has the potential for long-term results. Evergreen content continues to attract and engage audiences over time, providing ongoing value.

• Adaptability to Trends and Changes: The digital landscape is constantly evolving. Content marketing allows businesses to adapt quickly to new trends, technologies, and consumer behaviors, enabling them to stay relevant and competitive.

In summary, content marketing has become a cornerstone of successful marketing strategies in the digital age, offering businesses a powerful means to connect with audiences, drive engagement, and achieve sustainable growth by delivering valuable and relevant content.

THE CORE PRINCIPLES AND OBJECTIVES OF CONTENT MARKETING

The core principles and objectives of content marketing revolve around creating valuable, relevant, and consistent content to attract, engage, and retain a specific audience. These principles guide the strategies and actions taken in content marketing campaigns:

Core Principles of Content Marketing:

• Audience-Centric Approach: Content marketing is centered around the needs, interests, and preferences of the target audience. Understanding the audience's pain points, motivations, and behaviors is crucial in creating content that resonates with them.

• Value and Relevance: Content should provide genuine value, whether it's in the form of information, entertainment, education, or solutions to problems. It should be relevant to the audience's interests and offer something meaningful to them.

• Consistency and Quality: Consistency in delivering high-quality content builds trust and credibility. Maintaining a standard of excellence across all content pieces reinforces the brand's reputation and keeps the audience engaged.

• Storytelling and Engagement: Compelling storytelling helps in capturing attention and engaging the audience emotionally. A well-crafted narrative can make the content more memorable and impactful.

• Multi-Channel Presence: Content marketing extends across various channels and formats to reach audiences where they are most active. It's important to adapt content to suit different platforms while maintaining a cohesive brand message.

Objectives of Content Marketing:

• Building Brand Awareness: Content marketing aims to increase visibility and recognition for the brand among the target audience, thereby expanding its reach and market presence.

• Driving Engagement and Audience Interaction: The primary objective is to engage the audience, encourage interactions, such as likes, shares, comments, and ultimately foster a community around the brand.

• Lead Generation and Conversion: Content marketing plays a role in the sales funnel by attracting leads through valuable content and nurturing them towards conversion through informative and persuasive content.

• Establishing Authority and Trust: By consistently providing valuable content, businesses aim to position themselves as industry leaders and trusted sources of information, fostering trust among their audience.

• Customer Retention and Loyalty: Content marketing contributes to retaining existing customers by continually providing them with valuable information and maintaining engagement, thus building long-term loyalty.

• SEO and Organic Traffic: Creating optimized content aids in improving search engine rankings, attracting organic traffic, and increasing the website's visibility online.

• Measurable Results and Analysis: Content marketing seeks to generate measurable results through key performance indicators (KPIs) such as engagement metrics, conversion rates, traffic, and other analytics, allowing for continuous improvement and optimization.

Overall, the core principles and objectives of content marketing focus on delivering value, building relationships, and achieving specific business goals by leveraging the power of content creation, distribution, and engagement.

Content marketing offers a multitude of benefits for businesses in today's digital landscape. Here are some key advantages:

• Increased Brand Visibility and Awareness: Publishing high-quality, relevant content helps businesses to gain visibility in search engines and across various online platforms. This increased visibility enhances brand recognition and awareness among the target audience.

• Enhanced Engagement and Audience Interaction: Engaging content attracts and captivates the audience, encouraging interactions such as likes, comments, shares, and discussions. This interaction fosters a sense of community and strengthens the relationship between the brand and its audience.

• Improved Customer Trust and Credibility: Consistently providing valuable content establishes the brand as a reliable and authoritative source within its industry. This builds trust with the audience, leading to increased credibility and loyalty among customers.

• Effective Lead Generation and Conversion: Valuable content attracts potential customers and guides them through the sales funnel. By offering informative and relevant content, businesses can nurture leads and eventually convert them into paying customers.

• Cost-Effectiveness Compared to Traditional Advertising: Content marketing is often more cost-effective than traditional advertising methods. Creating content, especially through digital channels, can reach a wider audience at a fraction of the cost of traditional advertising.

• SEO Benefits and Increased Website Traffic: Well-optimized content contributes to better search engine rankings. By utilizing relevant keywords and providing valuable information, content marketing helps increase organic traffic to the website.

• Long-Term and Evergreen Value: Quality content has a lasting impact. Evergreen content continues to attract and engage audiences over time, providing ongoing value without expiration.

• Ability to Showcase Expertise and Thought Leadership: By sharing valuable insights, expertise, and industry knowledge through content, businesses can establish themselves as thought leaders in their respective fields, gaining respect and authority among peers and customers.

• Versatility and Adaptability Across Platforms: Content marketing allows businesses to leverage various content formats (blogs, videos, podcasts, infographics, etc.) and adapt to different platforms, catering to diverse audience preferences and behaviors.

• Measurable Results and Data-Driven Insights: Content marketing efforts can be measured through various analytics tools, providing valuable insights into audience behavior, preferences, and content performance. This data allows for continuous improvement and optimization of content strategies.

Overall, content marketing offers a wealth of benefits, empowering businesses to connect with their audience, drive engagement, and achieve their marketing objectives in a cost-effective and impactful manner.

DIFFERENCES BETWEEN CONTENT MARKETING AND TRADITIONAL ADVERTISING

Content marketing and traditional advertising are two distinct approaches to reaching and engaging an audience. Here are the key differences between them:

Content Marketing:

• Focus on Value and Education: Content marketing revolves around creating valuable, informative, and relevant content that addresses the audience's needs, interests, or pain points. It aims to provide value to the audience rather than focusing solely on promotional messages.

• Relationship Building: Content marketing emphasizes building relationships and trust with the audience over time. It aims to engage and connect with the audience by offering meaningful content that resonates with them.

• Customer-Centric Approach: The primary focus of content marketing is on the audience. It aims to attract and retain customers by addressing their concerns, offering solutions, and guiding them through the buyer's journey.

• Two-Way Communication: Content marketing often encourages two-way communication and engagement. It invites interaction through comments, shares, discussions, and feedback, fostering a community around the brand.

• Long-Term and Evergreen Value: Quality content in content marketing often retains its value over time. Evergreen content continues to provide value and attract audiences long after it's been published.

• Varied Content Formats: Content marketing employs various formats such as blog posts, videos, podcasts, infographics, eBooks, etc., adapting to diverse audience preferences and consumption habits.

Traditional Advertising:

• Promotional Messaging: Traditional advertising predominantly focuses on promoting products or services through paid advertisements. It aims to persuade or influence the audience to make a purchase or take immediate action.

• Brand Exposure and Awareness: Traditional advertising seeks to create brand awareness and exposure through mass media channels like TV, radio, print, billboards, etc., often using one-way communication methods.

• Short-Term Impact: Traditional advertising campaigns often have a shorter lifespan and immediate impact. They aim to capture attention and drive immediate sales or actions.

• Limited Interaction: Traditional advertising typically has limited interaction with the audience. It's a one-way communication where the audience receives the message without active participation or engagement.

• Higher Costs and Specific Channels: Traditional advertising can be costly, especially for prime-time TV slots or full-page print ads. It usually relies on specific advertising channels with set costs.

• Focused on Product/Service Promotion: The primary goal of traditional advertising is to showcase products or services and persuade consumers to buy, rather than to educate or provide in-depth information.

In summary, while traditional advertising focuses on direct promotion and short-term impact through paid advertisements, content marketing prioritizes delivering value, building relationships, and engaging audiences with valuable content over the long term.

THE STAGES OF CONTENT MARKETING

Content marketing involves various stages, each crucial for creating, distributing, and optimizing content to achieve marketing goals. These stages form a continuous cycle, allowing for refinement and improvement over time. Here are the key stages in content marketing:

1. Strategy and Planning:

• Goal Definition: Identify specific, measurable goals aligned with broader marketing objectives, such as increasing brand awareness, generating leads, or driving conversions.

• Audience Research: Conduct thorough research to understand the target audience's demographics, preferences, behaviors, pain points, and needs. Develop detailed buyer personas to guide content creation.

• Content Strategy Development: Create a comprehensive content strategy outlining the types of content, topics, formats, channels, and publishing schedules to reach and engage the target audience effectively.

2. Content Creation:

• Ideation and Planning: Brainstorm content ideas based on audience interests, industry trends, keyword research, and identified gaps in existing content. Plan content that aligns with the overall strategy.

• Content Development: Produce high-quality content that provides value to the audience. This may include articles, blog posts, videos, infographics, podcasts, eBooks, case studies, etc.

• SEO Optimization: Ensure content is optimized for search engines by using relevant keywords, meta tags, and a strong SEO strategy to improve visibility and attract organic traffic.

3. Content Distribution:

• Multi-Channel Distribution: Share content across various platforms such as social media, company blog, email newsletters, YouTube, LinkedIn, etc., considering where the target audience is most active.

• Promotion Strategies: Use promotional tactics like paid advertising, influencer collaborations, guest posting, and content syndication to increase reach and engagement.

• Content Calendar and Scheduling: Create a content calendar to plan and schedule content distribution systematically, maintaining consistency and ensuring content aligns with marketing goals.

4. Audience Engagement:

• Encouraging Interaction: Respond promptly to comments, messages, and feedback. Encourage audience participation, discussions, and user-generated content to foster a sense of community.

• Monitoring and Analytics: Monitor content performance using analytics tools to track metrics such as views, engagement, shares, conversions, and other key performance indicators (KPIs). Analyze data to refine strategies.

5. Evaluation and Optimization:

• Performance Analysis: Assess content performance against set goals and KPIs. Identify successful content and areas needing improvement based on data-driven insights.

• Iterative Improvement: Refine content strategies based on analysis. Adjust content types, distribution channels, messaging, or timing to optimize performance and better resonate with the audience.

• Testing and Experimentation: Experiment with different content formats, headlines, visuals, and calls-to-action (CTAs) to understand what works best and continuously improve.

6. Repurposing and Updating:

• Content Repurposing: Repurpose successful content into different formats or for different platforms to reach new audiences. For instance, turn a blog post into a video or create an eBook from multiple blog articles.

• Content Maintenance: Update and refresh older content to ensure relevance, accuracy, and continued value. This helps in maintaining search engine rankings and staying current with audience needs.

By following these stages and continuously iterating based on insights and feedback, content marketers can create an effective and evolving content strategy that resonates with their audience and achieves marketing objectives.

THE BUYER'S JOURNEY AND HOW CONTENT FITS INTO EACH STAGES

The buyer's journey refers to the stages that a potential customer goes through before making a purchase decision. It typically consists of three main phases:

Awareness, Consideration, and Decision. Content plays a crucial role in each stage of this journey by addressing the needs and concerns of the buyer at different points in their decision-making process.

1. Awareness Stage:

• Objective: At this stage, the buyer realizes they have a problem or need but might not have identified a specific solution yet.

• Content Role: Content aims to educate and raise awareness about the problem or need, positioning the brand as a helpful resource without explicitly promoting products or services.

Types of Content:

• Educational Blog Posts: Articles addressing common pain points or challenges faced by the audience.

• Infographics or Explainer Videos: Visual content providing insights into industry trends or offering general information.

• Guides and How-to Content: Step-by-step guides or tutorials related to the problem the audience faces.

2. Consideration Stage:

• Objective: The buyer is actively researching and considering different solutions to address their problem or need.

• Content Role: Content should offer more detailed information about potential solutions, highlighting the benefits and drawbacks to help the buyer evaluate options.

Types of Content:

• Product Comparisons: Content comparing different products or services within the industry.

• Case Studies or Whitepapers: In-depth analysis showcasing how the brand's solution has helped others.

• Webinars or Demonstrations: Interactive content demonstrating the use and effectiveness of the product or service.

3. Decision Stage:

• Objective: The buyer has narrowed down their options and is ready to make a purchase decision.

• Content Role: Content should provide the final push, emphasizing why the brand's solution is the best choice and addressing concerns or objections.

• Testimonials and Reviews: User-generated content or testimonials showcasing positive experiences with the brand.

• Free Trials or Demos: Offering trials or demos to allow the buyer to experience the product or service firsthand.

• Discounts or Special Offers: Providing incentives or exclusive deals to encourage purchase decisions.

Content Alignment with the Buyer's Journey:

• Tailoring Content: Create content specifically addressing the needs and questions of the buyer at each stage of their journey.

• Personalization: Use data and insights to personalize content delivery, offering relevant information based on the buyer's behavior and preferences.

• Consistent Messaging: Ensure consistency in brand messaging throughout the journey, building trust and familiarity with the buyer.

Content that aligns with the buyer's journey helps guide potential customers through the stages, providing valuable information and influencing their decision-making process. By understanding the buyer's needs at each stage, content marketers can create a strategic mix of content that effectively engages and converts leads into customers.

HOW TO DEFINE CLEAR AND ACHIEVABLE CONTENT MARKETING GOALS

Defining clear and achievable content marketing goals is essential for guiding your strategy, measuring success, and aligning efforts with broader business objectives. Here's a detailed process to define such goals:

1. Align with Business Objectives:

Understand Business Objectives: Start by comprehensively understanding the overarching goals of the business. Whether it's increasing sales, brand awareness, customer retention, lead generation, or market expansion, content marketing goals should directly support these objectives.

2. Make Goals Specific, Measurable, Attainable, Relevant, and Time-Bound (SMART):

Specific: Clearly articulate what you want to achieve. For instance, instead of a vague goal like "increase website traffic," specify, "increase organic website traffic by 30% within six months."

Measurable: Identify metrics or Key Performance Indicators (KPIs) to measure progress and success. Examples include website visits, engagement rates, conversions, lead generation, or sales attributed to content.

Achievable: Ensure that the goals are realistic and feasible within the given resources, capabilities, and timeframe. Set challenging but attainable targets that motivate your team.

Relevant: Goals should align with the broader business objectives and contribute directly to its success. They should be relevant to the audience and the content strategy.

Time-Bound: Set a clear timeline or deadline for achieving these goals. For instance, set quarterly or annual targets to track progress and assess success within a defined timeframe.

3. Use the 'Hierarchy of Goals' Approach:

Primary Goals: Identify primary overarching goals that align with the business, such as increasing brand awareness or driving sales.

Secondary Goals: Break down primary goals into more specific secondary goals. For instance, under 'increasing brand awareness,' you might have goals for website traffic, social media engagement, or email subscribers.

Tertiary Goals: Further break down secondary goals into specific actionable targets. For example, under 'increasing website traffic,' you might aim to increase organic traffic, referral traffic, and direct traffic by specific percentages.

4. Prioritize and Focus:

Prioritize Goals: Prioritize goals based on their importance to the business objectives. Focus on a few key goals at a time to avoid spreading resources too thinly.

5. Consider the Buyer's Journey:

Align Goals with the Buyer's Journey: Ensure that the content marketing goals correspond to different stages of the buyer's journey — awareness, consideration, and decision-making — to guide potential customers effectively.

6. Document and Communicate Goals:

Document Goals: Write down your content marketing goals in a concise and clear manner. Use a framework or template to document goals, KPIs, and associated metrics.

Communication and Alignment: Communicate these goals across the team, ensuring everyone understands and is aligned with the objectives. This fosters collaboration and ensures everyone works towards achieving the same targets.

7. Review and Adjust:

Regular Evaluation: Regularly review progress against these goals, analyze data, and reassess if needed. Adjust goals based on performance, market changes, or shifts in business priorities.

By following these steps, you can define clear, measurable, and achievable content marketing goals that support broader business objectives, guide your strategy, and enable effective measurement of success.

THE IMPORTANCE OF ALIGNING CONTENT WITH THE TARGET AUDIENCE'S NEEDS AND INTERESTS.

Aligning content with the needs and interests of the target audience is crucial for the success of content marketing strategies. Here's an in-depth look at why this alignment is so important:

1. Builds Trust and Credibility:

Understanding Audience Pain Points: When content directly addresses the challenges, problems, or questions that the audience faces, it demonstrates a deep understanding of their needs. This builds trust as they perceive the brand as knowledgeable and empathetic to their concerns.

2. Enhances Relevance and Engagement:

Capturing Attention: Content that resonates with the audience's interests is more likely to grab their attention. It compels them to engage, share, and interact with the content, leading to increased visibility and brand awareness.

3. Drives Audience-Centric Approach:

Customer-Centricity: Tailoring content to audience needs shifts the focus from merely selling products or services to providing value. It places the audience at the center of marketing efforts, emphasizing their satisfaction and fulfillment.

4. Guides Decision-Making and Purchase Intent:

Educating and Guiding: Content that addresses specific needs or offers solutions helps potential customers in their decision-making process. It guides them through the buyer's journey, influencing their purchasing decisions positively.

5. Strengthens Brand-Audience Relationships:

Fostering Connection: Relevant content establishes a meaningful connection between the brand and its audience. When the content consistently adds value to their lives, it cultivates a sense of loyalty and affinity towards the brand.

6. Increases Conversion Rates:

Higher Conversion Potential: Content aligned with audience needs is more likely to resonate with them emotionally or intellectually. This resonance increases the likelihood of converting leads into customers or encouraging repeat purchases.

7. Improves SEO and Organic Traffic:

Enhanced Search Visibility: When content addresses specific audience queries or interests, it tends to perform better in search engine results. This drives organic traffic as the content becomes more discoverable.

8. Enables Personalization and Customization:

Customized Experiences: Understanding audience needs allows for personalized content experiences. Tailored content based on demographics, behaviors, or preferences creates a more personalized journey for each audience segment.

9. Facilitates Effective Content Distribution:

Optimized Distribution Channels: Knowing audience preferences helps in selecting the right channels and formats for content distribution. It ensures that content reaches the audience where they are most active and engaged.

10. Encourages Long-Term Engagement:

Sustained Engagement: Content that consistently meets audience needs nurtures long-term relationships. It encourages ongoing engagement and interaction, fostering loyalty and advocacy for the brand.

In summary, aligning content with the needs and interests of the target audience forms the foundation of successful content marketing. It is instrumental in fostering connections, driving engagement, guiding purchasing decisions, and ultimately, building a loyal and satisfied customer base.

EXAMPLES OF SMART GOALS

SMART goals are specific, measurable, achievable, relevant, and time-bound objectives that provide clarity and direction for achieving desired outcomes. Here are examples of SMART goals across various areas:

Marketing:

• Specific: Increase website traffic by improving organic search rankings.

• Measurable: Achieve a 25% increase in organic traffic within six months.

• Achievable: Implement SEO best practices, content optimization, and link-building strategies.

• Relevant: Aligns with the goal of boosting brand visibility and attracting more potential customers.

• Time-Bound: Attain the traffic increase by the end of the third quarter.

Sales:

• Specific: Increase sales revenue from a specific product line.

• Measurable: Achieve a 15% increase in sales for the product line within the next quarter.

• Achievable: Launch targeted marketing campaigns, offer discounts, and improve product positioning.

• Relevant: Supports the overall revenue and profitability goals of the company.

• Time-Bound: Attain the sales increase by the end of the current fiscal quarter.

Human Resources:

• Specific: Improve employee retention rates.

• Measurable: Reduce employee turnover by 20% in the upcoming year.

• Achievable: Implement employee engagement programs, conduct satisfaction surveys, and offer professional development opportunities.

• Relevant: Enhances company culture, productivity, and long-term stability.

• Time-Bound: Achieve the reduction in turnover within the next fiscal year.

Project Management:

• Specific: Complete the development of a new software feature.

• Measurable: Finish coding and testing the new feature within eight weeks.

• Achievable: Allocate necessary resources, assign tasks, and adhere to the project timeline.

• Relevant: Aligns with customer demands and enhances the software's functionality.

• Time-Bound: Complete the feature development by the end of the two-month sprint.

Personal Development:

• Specific: Improve proficiency in a foreign language.

• Measurable: Achieve an intermediate level proficiency (B1) within nine months.

• Achievable: Devote 30 minutes daily to language practice, enroll in language courses, and engage in regular conversation practice.

• Relevant: Enhances communication skills for personal and professional growth.

• Time-Bound: Attain the intermediate proficiency level within nine months through consistent practice.

These SMART goal examples illustrate the importance of setting specific, measurable, achievable, relevant, and time-bound objectives across different domains to achieve desired outcomes effectively.

CHAPTER TWO

THE SIGNIFICANCE OF AUDIENCE PERSONAS

Audience personas, also known as buyer personas, are semi-fictional representations of your ideal customers based on market research, data, and insights about your existing customers. These personas represent different segments of your target audience and play a significant role in shaping various aspects of a business's strategies. Here's why audience personas are essential:

1. Understanding the Audience:

Detailed Insights: Personas provide in-depth information about the target audience's demographics, behaviors, goals, pain points, motivations, and preferences.

2. Targeted Content Creation:

Tailored Messaging: Helps in crafting content that resonates with specific audience segments, addressing their needs and interests at different stages of the buyer's journey.

Relevance and Engagement: Enables the creation of highly relevant and personalized content, leading to increased engagement and better response from the audience.

3. Improved Marketing Strategies:

Targeted Marketing: Guides marketing efforts by directing resources to the most relevant channels and messaging strategies for each persona, maximizing the effectiveness of campaigns.

Customized Approach: Allows for a more customized approach in advertising, email marketing, social media, and other promotional activities.

4. Product Development and Innovation:

Informed Product Decisions: Helps in understanding what features, benefits, or solutions are most important to different segments of the audience, guiding product development.

Innovation Insights: Provides insights into unmet needs or pain points of different personas, potentially sparking innovation for new products or services.

5. Enhancing Customer Experience:

Personalized Experience: Enables businesses to create a personalized and customer-centric experience across various touchpoints, fostering stronger relationships with customers.

Customer Service Improvement: Helps in understanding customer expectations and improving customer service based on each persona's unique preferences and behaviors.

6. Effective Communication:

Consistent Messaging: Ensures a consistent and unified brand message that aligns with the interests and needs of different audience segments, reducing confusion and reinforcing brand identity.

7. Targeted Sales Efforts:

Focused Sales Approach: Aids sales teams by providing insights into the pain points and motivations of different personas, allowing for more targeted and effective sales pitches.

8. Data-Driven Decision-Making:

Data Utilization: Guides decision-making based on data and insights rather than assumptions or generalizations, increasing the likelihood of successful strategies.

9. Adaptability and Flexibility:

Adapting to Changes: Allows businesses to adapt quickly to changing market trends, behaviors, or preferences of different segments by revising personas accordingly.

Overall, audience personas are crucial for businesses as they provide a deep understanding of the target audience, enabling tailored strategies that resonate with specific segments, leading to improved customer satisfaction, better engagement, and ultimately, business growth and success.

HOW TO CREATE AUDIENCE PERSONAS

Creating audience personas involves a detailed process of gathering data, analyzing insights, and synthesizing information to construct semi-fictional representations of your ideal customers. Here's a step-by-step guide on how to create audience personas:

1. Conduct Research:

Utilize Existing Data: Start by gathering data from various sources such as customer surveys, interviews, website analytics, social media insights, and sales data.

Analyze Customer Data: Review demographic information, behaviors, preferences, purchase history, pain points, motivations, and any other relevant information about your existing customers.

2. Identify Patterns and Commonalities:

Segmentation: Group customers into segments based on similarities in behavior, characteristics, needs, or preferences.

Identify Trends: Look for recurring themes, patterns, or trends within the data that can help distinguish different types of customers.

3. Create Persona Profiles:

Name and Details: Give each persona a name and relevant details to make them more personable and relatable. Include demographics (age, gender, location, job title), interests, behaviors, goals, challenges, and values.

Develop Scenarios: Describe scenarios or situations that illustrate how each persona interacts with your product or service. Include their needs, pain points, and motivations at different stages of their journey.

4. Validate and Refine:

Validation: Validate personas by comparing them with real customer data or by conducting additional interviews or surveys to ensure accuracy.

Refinement: Refine personas based on feedback and insights obtained, adjusting details or characteristics to better align with real audience segments.

5. Use Persona Templates or Frameworks:

Templates: Utilize predefined templates or frameworks designed for creating personas. These often include sections for demographics, goals, challenges, behaviors, and quotes representing each persona.

6. Assign Priorities:

Priority Personas: Identify primary, secondary, and tertiary personas based on their relevance and impact on your business objectives.

7. Disseminate and Utilize:

Share and Utilize: Share personas with relevant teams (marketing, sales, product development) to ensure alignment across departments. Use personas to guide content creation, marketing strategies, product development, and customer service initiatives.

8. Continuously Update and Evolve:

Regular Review: Regularly review and update personas based on evolving market trends, changes in customer behaviors, or new data insights.

Tools for Creating Personas:

• Persona Creation Tools: Several online tools (such as HubSpot's Make My Persona, Xtensio, or UserForge) offer templates and tools specifically designed for creating audience personas, streamlining the process.

By following these steps and utilizing available data and insights, businesses can create comprehensive audience personas that accurately represent their target customers. These personas serve as valuable tools for aligning strategies, improving customer engagement, and driving business success.

HOW TO CONDUCT AUDIENCE RESEARCH AND UNDERSTAND THEIR NEEDS, PAIN POINTS AND PREFERENCES

Conducting audience research to understand their needs, pain points, and preferences involves a strategic process of data collection, analysis, and interpretation. Here's a detailed guide on how to conduct effective audience research:

1. Define Research Objectives:

Clear Objectives: Determine what specific information you aim to gather about your audience. Define goals related to understanding their needs, pain points, preferences, and behaviors.

2. Utilize Various Data Sources:

• Customer Surveys and Interviews: Create surveys or conduct interviews with your existing customers or target audience. Ask about their preferences, challenges, motivations, and experiences related to your product or industry.

• Website Analytics: Analyze website data to understand visitor behavior, popular pages, time spent, and navigation patterns. Identify the content that resonates most with your audience.

• Social Media Insights: Use social media analytics to understand audience demographics, engagement metrics, and sentiment analysis. Monitor discussions, comments, and feedback related to your industry or brand.

• Sales and CRM Data: Analyze sales data, customer feedback, and interactions with customer relationship management (CRM) tools to understand purchasing behavior, preferences, and pain points.

3. Create Buyer Surveys and Questionnaires:

Targeted Surveys: Develop surveys or questionnaires tailored to gather specific information about your audience's preferences, needs, and challenges.

Open-Ended Questions: Include open-ended questions to allow respondents to provide detailed insights and express their thoughts freely.

4. Conduct Interviews and Focus Groups:

One-on-One Interviews: Conduct interviews with individuals representing your target audience. Ask probing questions to gather qualitative data and understand their perspectives deeply.

Focus Groups: Organize focus group sessions to discuss specific topics or issues. Engage participants in discussions to gain diverse opinions and insights.

5. Analyze Data and Extract Insights:

Data Analysis: Analyze the collected data to identify patterns, trends, common pain points, preferences, and behaviors among your audience segments.

Quantitative vs. Qualitative Analysis: Combine quantitative data (numbers, metrics) with qualitative data (opinions, sentiments) to form a comprehensive understanding.

6. Build Empathy Maps or User Personas:

Empathy Mapping: Create empathy maps that visualize your audience's thoughts, feelings, pain points, motivations, and behaviors.

User Personas: Develop detailed user personas that represent different segments of your audience, incorporating insights gained from research.

7. Test and Validate Findings:

Validation and Testing: Validate your research findings by cross-referencing data, conducting additional surveys or interviews, and testing assumptions to ensure accuracy.

8. Implement Insights in Strategies:

Strategy Alignment: Utilize the gathered insights to inform content creation, product development, marketing strategies, customer service initiatives, and overall business decisions.

9. Continuously Update and Evolve:

Continuous Monitoring: Regularly monitor and update your understanding of the audience to stay abreast of changing needs, preferences, and market trends.

By following these steps and leveraging various data sources, businesses can gain a comprehensive understanding of their audience's needs, pain points, and preferences. This information is invaluable for tailoring products, services, and marketing efforts to better meet audience expectations and drive business growth.

A content strategy is crucial for businesses as it serves as a roadmap that outlines how content will be planned, created, published, and managed to meet specific business goals and resonate with the target audience. Here's why having a content strategy is important:

1. Aligns with Business Goals:

Strategic Alignment: Helps align content efforts with overall business objectives, ensuring that content supports and contributes to broader organizational goals such as brand awareness, lead generation, sales, or customer retention.

2. Audience-Centric Approach:

Understanding Audience Needs: Enables businesses to understand their audience better, catering to their needs, preferences, pain points, and interests through tailored content. This fosters stronger relationships and engagement.

3. Consistency and Branding:

Consistent Messaging: Ensures consistent brand messaging and tone across all content channels, reinforcing brand identity and values.

Brand Visibility: Maintains a steady flow of content that keeps the brand visible and relevant to the target audience.

4. Improves Content Effectiveness:

Strategic Planning: Guides the creation of relevant and valuable content at each stage of the buyer's journey, ensuring content aligns with audience needs at different touchpoints.

Optimized Content: Helps in optimizing content for search engines (SEO), ensuring better visibility and reach.

5. Efficient Resource Allocation:

Resource Management: Helps allocate resources (time, budget, human resources) effectively by focusing efforts on content types, channels, and topics that deliver the most impact.

6. Enhanced User Experience:

Valuable Content: Provides users with valuable and meaningful content that educates, entertains, or solves their problems, enhancing their experience with the brand.

7. Measurable Results and Adaptability:

Data-Driven Approach: Allows for tracking and measurement of content performance against predetermined KPIs, enabling informed decision-making based on data insights.

Adaptation and Improvement: Provides a framework for continuous improvement, allowing strategies to be refined based on performance data and audience feedback.

8. Integrated Marketing Efforts:

Collaborative Efforts: Encourages collaboration among different departments (marketing, sales, customer service) to ensure a consistent and integrated approach to customer communication and engagement.

9. Long-Term Sustainability:

Scalability and Longevity: Provides a structured plan that can evolve and adapt to changing market conditions, ensuring sustainability in the long run.

10. Competitive Advantage:

Stand Out from Competition: A well-defined content strategy can differentiate a brand by offering unique and valuable content, setting it apart from competitors.

In summary, a content strategy is essential for businesses as it serves as a guiding framework that not only ensures the creation of valuable and relevant content but also aligns content efforts with business objectives, audience needs, and evolving market trends, ultimately driving growth, engagement, and success.

HOW TO CREATE A CONTENT STRATEGY

Creating a content strategy involves a structured process that outlines how content will be planned, created, published, and managed to achieve specific business goals. Here are steps to create an effective content strategy:

1. Define Objectives and Audience:

Set Clear Goals: Define specific and measurable objectives such as increasing brand awareness, driving website traffic, generating leads, boosting sales, or improving customer retention.

Identify Target Audience: Understand your audience's demographics, behaviors, preferences, pain points, and interests. Create buyer personas representing different segments of your audience.

2. Conduct Content Audit and Analysis:

Content Inventory: Review existing content assets to identify gaps, strengths, weaknesses, and areas for improvement.

Audience Analysis: Analyze audience data to understand which types of content resonate most with your audience and perform well across various channels.

3. Establish Key Performance Indicators (KPIs):

Identify Metrics: Determine key metrics aligned with your objectives. These may include website traffic, engagement rates, conversion rates, leads generated, or social media metrics.

4. Content Ideation and Planning:

Content Calendar: Create a content calendar outlining topics, formats, and publishing schedules aligned with audience preferences and buyer personas.

Content Types and Channels: Determine the types of content (blogs, videos, infographics, webinars, podcasts, etc.) suitable for conveying your messages. Choose appropriate distribution channels (website, social media, email, etc.).

5. Content Creation and Optimization:

Quality Content: Develop high-quality, valuable, and engaging content that addresses audience needs, pain points, and interests.

SEO and Keywords: Incorporate SEO strategies and relevant keywords to improve search engine visibility and reach.

6. Distribution and Promotion:

Content Promotion Strategy: Plan how content will be promoted across various channels to reach the target audience effectively. Utilize social media, email marketing, influencer collaborations, and paid advertising where relevant.

7. Monitor and Measure:

Analytics and Tracking: Use analytics tools to measure content performance against established KPIs. Monitor metrics regularly to assess content effectiveness.

Iterative Improvement: Analyze data insights and audience feedback to make informed adjustments and improvements to the content strategy continuously.

8. Resource Allocation and Team Collaboration:

Resource Management: Allocate resources such as budget, time, and personnel to support the content strategy effectively.

Cross-Team Collaboration: Foster collaboration among different departments (marketing, sales, customer service) to ensure an integrated approach and consistency in messaging.

9. Review and Adapt:

Regular Review: Conduct regular reviews of the content strategy to ensure it remains aligned with business goals, audience needs, and industry trends. Adapt strategies based on changing circumstances.

10. Documentation and Communication:

Document Strategy: Create a detailed content strategy document outlining objectives, audience insights, content plans, schedules, and KPIs. Share this document with relevant stakeholders for alignment and understanding.

By following these steps, businesses can create a comprehensive and effective content strategy that aligns with their goals, resonates with their audience, and drives success in their marketing efforts.

VARIOUS CONTENT FORMATS

Content formats refer to the diverse types of content that can be created and shared across different platforms to engage audiences. Here are various content formats widely used in marketing and content creation:

1. Blogs and Articles:

Description: Informative, educational, or entertaining written content typically published on websites. They cover diverse topics and can vary in length and style.

Use: Educate audiences, address specific topics, provide insights, and improve SEO by targeting relevant keywords.

2. Videos:

Description: Visual content ranging from short clips to longer-form videos. It includes explainer videos, tutorials, vlogs, interviews, webinars, and more.

Use: Engage audiences visually, demonstrate products/services, convey complex information, and foster brand personality.

3. Infographics:

Description: Visual representations combining text, graphics, and data to explain complex information or statistics in a visually appealing and easy-to-understand format.

Use: Summarize data, illustrate processes, and communicate information quickly and effectively.

4. Podcasts:

Description: Audio content, often episodic, covering various topics or discussions. It can include interviews, storytelling, educational content, or entertainment.

Use: Reach audiences on-the-go, share expertise, entertain, and build a loyal listener base.

5. E-books and Whitepapers:

Description: Long-form written content presented in a downloadable PDF format. E-books are often less formal, whereas whitepapers are detailed reports addressing specific issues or topics.

Use: Offer in-depth information, share research findings, generate leads through gated content.

6. Social Media Posts:

Description: Short-form content tailored for social media platforms such as Facebook, Twitter, Instagram, LinkedIn, etc. It includes text, images, videos, stories, polls, and more.

Use: Engage audiences, build communities, share updates, and drive traffic to websites or other content.

7. Webinars and Live Streaming:

Description: Live or pre-recorded interactive sessions, workshops, or presentations conducted online. They allow real-time engagement and Q&A sessions.

Use: Educate audiences, demonstrate products, provide training, and engage with viewers in real-time.

8. Interactive Content:

Description: Engaging content formats that require user interaction, such as quizzes, polls, calculators, surveys, interactive maps, etc.

Use: Boost engagement, gather user data, provide personalized experiences, and increase time spent on content.

9. User-Generated Content (UGC):

Description: Content created by users, customers, or followers, such as reviews, testimonials, social media posts, or submissions.

Use: Build trust, authenticity, and social proof by showcasing real experiences and opinions of customers.

10. Case Studies and Testimonials:

Description: Detailed accounts of successful projects, experiences, or outcomes showcasing how products or services benefited specific clients or customers.

Use: Demonstrate credibility, showcase success stories, and provide evidence of your offerings' value.

11. Email Newsletters:

Description: Regularly scheduled emails containing curated content, updates, offers, and information tailored for subscribers.

Use: Nurture leads, maintain engagement, deliver personalized content, and drive traffic to websites or specific actions.

Each content format serves a unique purpose and caters to different audience preferences. Combining various formats within a content strategy can help businesses effectively engage and connect with their audiences across different platforms and stages of the buyer's journey.

CONTENT TYPES

Content types refer to specific categories or classifications of content that serve different purposes, formats, and objectives in a content strategy. Here's an overview of various content types commonly used in marketing and digital media:

Informational Content:

• Blogs/Articles: Written content providing information, insights, or opinions on specific topics.

• E-books/Whitepapers: Long-form content offering comprehensive information or research findings.

• Guides/Tutorials: Step-by-step instructions or how-to guides for specific tasks or subjects.

• FAQs: Answers to frequently asked questions about products, services, or topics.

Visual Content:

• Images/Graphics: Visual representations used to convey messages or support content.

• Infographics: Visual representations combining text and graphics to present complex information.

• Memes: Humorous or viral images with a message, often shared on social media.

• Presentations/Slideshares: Visual presentations used for sharing information or insights.

Video and Audio Content:

• Videos: Visual content in various formats (explainers, tutorials, interviews, vlogs, etc.).

• Podcasts: Audio content in episodic formats covering discussions, interviews, or stories.

Interactive Content:

• Quizzes/Polls/Surveys: Engaging content formats that require user interaction.

• Calculators/Tools: Interactive tools allowing users to perform specific calculations or tasks.

Social Media Content:

• Posts/Updates: Content shared on social media platforms (text, images, videos, stories, etc.).

• Live Streaming: Real-time video broadcasts on social platforms engaging with audiences.

• User-Generated Content (UGC): Content created and shared by users or customers (reviews, testimonials, etc.).

Sales and Marketing Content:

• Case Studies/Testimonials: Detailed accounts showcasing successful experiences or outcomes.

• Product Demos/Reviews: Presentations or reviews demonstrating product features or benefits.

• Sales Collaterals: Brochures, flyers, or sales presentations used for marketing purposes.

Email Marketing Content:

• Newsletters: Regularly scheduled emails containing updates, offers, or curated content.

• Drip Campaigns: Automated series of emails sent based on user actions or schedules.

PR and Communication Content:

• Press Releases: Official announcements or news shared with the media or public.

• Company Reports: Annual reports, financial statements, or performance reports.

Each content type serves a specific purpose within a content strategy, targeting different stages of the buyer's journey or fulfilling varied business objectives. Integrating a mix of these content types helps businesses effectively engage their audience, convey their messages, and achieve their marketing and communication goals.

CONTENT CALENDAR CREATION

Creating a content calendar involves planning and scheduling content creation, publication dates, and distribution across various platforms. It helps maintain consistency, organize efforts, and align content with business goals and audience preferences. Here's a step-by-step guide to creating a content calendar:

1. Define Goals and Audience:

Set Objectives: Determine the purpose of your content (e.g., increasing brand awareness, driving traffic, generating leads).

Understand Audience: Identify your target audience's preferences, behaviors, and needs.

2. Choose a Format and Tools:

Select a Calendar Format: Use spreadsheets, project management tools (like Asana, Trello), or specialized content calendar software.

Choose Tools: Select tools that suit your team's needs for planning, scheduling, and collaboration.

3. List Content Ideas and Topics:

Brainstorm Ideas: Generate a list of potential content topics aligned with your objectives and audience preferences.

Consider Varieties: Include different content types (blogs, videos, infographics) that cater to various audience preferences.

4. Establish Content Themes and Categories:

Define Themes: Group content topics into themes or categories. For example, educational content, industry insights, customer stories, etc.

Diversify: Ensure a balanced mix of content types and themes to maintain audience interest.

5. Determine Publishing Frequency and Timing:

Frequency: Decide how often you'll publish content (daily, weekly, bi-weekly, etc.), considering resources and audience engagement.

Timing: Identify optimal times and days for posting content based on audience behavior and platform insights.

6. Create a Calendar Template:

Calendar Structure: Design a calendar template with columns for content titles, types, themes, publication dates, channels, and responsible team members.

Include Details: Add relevant details like keywords, call-to-actions, and links.

7. Plan Content Creation and Distribution:

Assign Tasks: Assign responsibilities to team members for content creation, editing, and publishing.

Plan Distribution: Schedule content distribution across various channels (social media, website, email, etc.) based on the calendar.

8. Review and Schedule Content:

Content Review: Ensure content aligns with brand guidelines, quality standards, and SEO best practices.

Scheduling: Populate the calendar with content titles, details, and scheduled publication dates.

9. Collaborate and Communicate:

Team Collaboration: Encourage collaboration among team members by sharing the content calendar and discussing ideas or revisions.

Communication: Ensure clear communication regarding deadlines, updates, and any changes in the content calendar.

10. Monitor and Update:

Regular Review: Continuously monitor content performance against set KPIs.

Adjustments: Update the calendar based on performance insights, audience feedback, or changes in business objectives.

A well-organized content calendar streamlines content creation and publication processes, maintains consistency, and helps teams stay focused on producing high-quality content that resonates with the target audience.

HOW TO CREATE A CONTENT CALENDAR AND MANAGE CONTENT PRODUCTION

Creating a content calendar and effectively managing content production is essential for maintaining consistency, staying organized, and meeting publishing deadlines in content marketing. Here's a step-by-step guide to creating a content calendar and managing content production:

1. Define Content Marketing Goals:

Establish Objectives: Determine the purpose and goals of your content strategy (e.g., brand awareness, lead generation, customer engagement).

Understand Audience: Identify your target audience's preferences, pain points, and interests.

2. Content Planning and Strategy:

Content Inventory: Take stock of existing content assets and their performance to identify gaps or areas for improvement.

Content Strategy Development: Create a content strategy outlining themes, topics, formats, and key messages aligned with your goals and audience needs.

3. Content Calendar Creation:

Select a Calendar Tool: Choose a suitable platform or tool (Google Calendar, Excel, Trello, Asana, CoSchedule) for creating your content calendar.

Calendar Structure: Define columns or sections for content topics, publishing dates, content types, distribution channels, keywords, and responsible team members.

4. Content Ideation and Scheduling:

Ideation Process: Brainstorm content ideas based on your content strategy, audience interests, trends, and industry insights.

Content Calendar Population: Populate your content calendar with planned topics, publication dates, and assigned responsible team members.

5. Align with Editorial and Campaign Calendars:

Coordinate Efforts: Align content calendar with editorial calendars, marketing campaigns, product launches, or seasonal events to ensure cohesive messaging and timing.

Integration with Campaigns: Incorporate campaign-specific content and promotional activities into the calendar.

6. Content Production Workflow:

Assign Responsibilities: Clearly define roles and responsibilities for content creation, including writers, designers, editors, and reviewers.

Establish Workflow: Develop a workflow outlining the content creation process from ideation to publishing, including review and approval stages.

7. Content Creation and Optimization:

Content Creation Guidelines: Develop style guides, templates, and standards for maintaining consistency across content pieces.

Optimization Practices: Ensure content is optimized for SEO, readability, and audience engagement based on best practices.

8. Review and Approval Processes:

Content Review: Set up a review and approval process to maintain content quality, accuracy, and adherence to brand guidelines.

Revision Cycle: Incorporate feedback loops and revision cycles to improve content before finalizing it for publishing.

9. Content Publishing and Distribution:

Scheduled Publishing: Use your content calendar to schedule publishing dates and times across various channels (blog, social media, email, etc.).

Cross-Promotion: Plan cross-promotion strategies to leverage content across multiple channels for maximum reach and impact.

10. Monitor, Measure, and Iterate:

Performance Tracking: Regularly monitor content performance using analytics tools and track key metrics outlined in your content strategy.

Analysis and Optimization: Analyze data insights to identify successful content and areas for improvement, then optimize future content accordingly.

11. Regular Updates and Iterations:

Review and Adjust: Conduct periodic reviews of your content calendar to assess its effectiveness and make necessary adjustments based on changing priorities, audience feedback, or market trends.

Iterative Improvement: Continually refine and evolve your content calendar and production processes to enhance efficiency and effectiveness over time.

By following these steps and maintaining a structured approach to content planning, creation, and scheduling, you can effectively manage content production, maintain consistency, and drive successful content marketing initiatives.

THE NEED FOR CONSISTENCY AND VARIETY IN CONTENT CREATION

Consistency and variety in content creation are both essential components of a successful content strategy, serving different yet equally important purposes:

Need for Consistency:

• Builds Trust and Reliability: Consistent content delivery establishes trust with your audience. When they know when and where to expect new content, it fosters reliability and loyalty.

• Reinforces Brand Identity: Consistent messaging, tone, and visual style across content reinforce your brand identity, making it more recognizable and memorable.

• Improves SEO and Visibility: Regularly published and consistent content signals to search engines that your website is active and relevant, potentially improving search engine rankings.

• Engagement and Audience Retention: Consistency keeps your audience engaged. Regular updates keep them returning for new information, updates, or entertainment, reducing the risk of losing interest.

• Optimizes Audience Engagement: Consistent posting schedules on social media or other platforms can increase audience engagement due to predictability.

Need for Variety:

• Maintains Audience Interest: Variety in content keeps your audience engaged. Diverse content types prevent monotony and cater to different preferences within your audience.

• Attracts Different Audience Segments: Various content formats appeal to different segments of your audience. Some may prefer videos, while others prefer articles or infographics.

• Covers Different Stages of Buyer's Journey: Different content types are effective at different stages of the buyer's journey. For example, informational blogs may attract new leads, while case studies might convert them into customers.

• Encourages Sharing and Reach: Diverse content encourages social sharing. Videos, infographics, or interactive content tend to be shared more frequently, extending your content's reach.

• Enhances SEO and Website Traffic: Offering diverse content improves dwell time on your website, reduces bounce rates, and increases the chances of getting backlinks, all of which positively impact SEO.

Balancing Consistency and Variety:

• Content Themes: Maintain consistency through recurring themes or topics while exploring various angles or perspectives within those themes.

• Content Mix: Use a mix of content types (blogs, videos, podcasts, infographics) while aligning them with your brand's tone and messaging.

• Editorial Calendar: Plan a consistent publishing schedule but incorporate diverse content types and topics within that schedule.

• Audience Feedback: Monitor audience engagement and feedback to understand which content types or topics resonate best. Adjust your strategy accordingly.

In summary, consistency builds trust and reliability, while variety ensures engagement and caters to diverse audience preferences. Balancing both aspects in your content strategy is key to effectively reaching and engaging your audience while maintaining a strong brand presence.

TECHNIQUES FOR GENERATING ENGAGING AND HIGH-qUALITY CONTENT

Generating engaging and high-quality content requires a strategic approach that focuses on audience needs, creativity, and relevance. Here are several techniques to create compelling content:

1. Understand Your Audience:

Audience Research: Conduct thorough audience research to understand their demographics, preferences, pain points, and interests.

Create Personas: Develop detailed buyer personas representing different segments of your audience to tailor content that resonates with them.

2. Focus on Valuable Content:

Provide Solutions: Address audience problems, questions, or needs by offering informative, educational, or entertaining content.

Originality and Uniqueness: Offer fresh perspectives, unique insights, or innovative ideas to distinguish your content from competitors.

3. Use Compelling Visuals:

Visual Appeal: Incorporate high-quality images, infographics, videos, or interactive elements to enhance content engagement.

Visual Storytelling: Utilize visuals to narrate stories or convey complex information in an easily digestible format.

4. Craft Captivating Headlines and Introductions:

Eye-Catching Headlines: Create attention-grabbing headlines that pique curiosity and compel readers to click.

Engaging Introductions: Start with compelling introductions that hook the audience and encourage them to continue reading.

5. Implement Storytelling Techniques:

Narrative Approach: Tell stories that evoke emotions, connect with readers, and illustrate key points.

Use Case Studies or Testimonials: Share real-life experiences or success stories that resonate with your audience.

6. Provide Actionable and Practical Advice:

How-To Guides or Tutorials: Offer step-by-step instructions or guides that help readers solve specific problems or learn new skills.

Checklists or Templates: Provide practical tools that readers can implement immediately.

7. Encourage Interaction and Engagement:

Interactive Content: Create quizzes, polls, surveys, or interactive tools that encourage user participation.

Encourage Comments and Feedback: Prompt readers to leave comments, share opinions, or ask questions, fostering engagement.

8. Optimize for Readability and SEO:

Formatting: Use bullet points, subheadings, and short paragraphs to improve readability.

SEO Best Practices: Incorporate relevant keywords, meta descriptions, and internal/external links for better search visibility.

9. Consistency in Publishing:

Regular Schedule: Maintain a consistent publishing schedule to keep audiences engaged and returning for new content.

Content Calendar: Plan and schedule content in advance to ensure a steady flow of fresh material.

10. Measure and Iterate:

Analytics Review: Use analytics tools to track content performance (engagement metrics, conversions, etc.).

Iterative Improvement: Analyze data insights to understand what works best and make adjustments to future content strategies.

By employing these techniques and continually refining your approach based on audience feedback and performance metrics, you can create content that resonates with your audience, drives engagement, and adds value to your brand.

CHAPTER THREE

THE IMPORTANCE OF SEO IN CONTENT MARKETING

Search Engine Optimization (SEO) plays a pivotal role in content marketing, contributing significantly to a brand's online visibility, organic traffic, and overall digital presence. Here's why SEO is crucial in content marketing:

1. Increased Online Visibility:

Improved Rankings: SEO-optimized content ranks higher in search engine results pages (SERPs), increasing visibility to potential audiences.

Enhanced Search Presence: Higher visibility means more chances for users to discover and engage with your content.

2. Drive Organic Traffic:

Targeted Traffic: SEO helps attract qualified and relevant traffic by targeting specific keywords and phrases that users are searching for.

Long-Term Traffic: Well-optimized content can continue to drive traffic over time, providing lasting value.

3. Better User Experience:

Optimized Content Structure: SEO practices encourage improved content structure, making it more readable, scannable, and user-friendly.

Mobile-Friendliness: SEO emphasizes mobile optimization, ensuring content is accessible across devices, which contributes to a positive user experience.

4. Credibility and Trust:

Authority Building: Higher rankings and visibility in search results can establish your brand as an authoritative source in your industry or niche.

Trustworthiness: Appearing in top search results can instill trust and credibility in the eyes of users, leading to higher click-through rates.

5. Content Relevance and Targeting:

Keyword Optimization: SEO guides content creators to use relevant keywords that align with user intent, ensuring content addresses audience needs.

Understanding User Intent: SEO practices focus on understanding what users are searching for and tailoring content to fulfill those needs.

6. Enhanced Content Performance:

Data-Driven Insights: SEO tools provide valuable insights into audience behavior, preferences, and content performance, enabling data-driven content strategies.

Continuous Improvement: SEO metrics and analytics help in refining content strategies for better performance over time.

7. Competitive Advantage:

Stay Ahead of Competitors: Effective SEO practices can help

businesses stay ahead of competitors by securing higher search rankings, attracting more traffic, and gaining more visibility.

Local SEO Advantage: For businesses targeting local audiences, local SEO tactics can improve visibility in local searches, giving an edge over competitors in the same geographical area.

8. Cost-Effectiveness and Long-Term Benefits:

Cost-Efficient Marketing: Organic search traffic gained through SEO efforts can be cost-effective compared to paid advertising.

Long-Term Results: Well-optimized content continues to drive traffic and results over time, offering long-term benefits compared to short-lived paid campaigns.

9. Adaptability to Evolving Trends:

Adapting to Algorithm Changes: SEO practices constantly evolve to match search engine algorithm updates, ensuring content remains optimized for current trends and best practices.

10. Integration with Overall Marketing Strategy:

Synergy with Other Channels: SEO complements and integrates with other marketing channels like social media, email marketing, and content distribution, creating a unified marketing strategy.

In summary, SEO is integral to content marketing as it improves online visibility, drives organic traffic, enhances user experience, establishes credibility, and provides valuable data insights. Incorporating SEO best practices into content creation ensures that content is not only discoverable but also relevant and valuable to the target audience, contributing to the overall success of a brand's digital marketing efforts.

KEYWORD RESEARCH

Keyword research is a critical component of SEO that involves identifying the words and phrases users enter into search engines when looking for information, products, or services. This process helps content creators and marketers understand what their target audience is searching for online. Here's how keyword research works:

1. Understanding the Importance:

Relevance: Identifying keywords relevant to your industry, niche, products, or services is crucial for attracting the right audience.

User Intent: Keywords reveal the intent behind searches, whether informational, navigational, commercial, or transactional.

2. Steps in Keyword Research:

Brainstorming: Start by brainstorming seed keywords - general terms related to your business, products, or services.

Keyword Expansion Tools: Use keyword research tools (e.g., Google Keyword Planner, SEMrush, Ahrefs, Moz) to expand your list by suggesting related keywords and providing data on search volumes, competition, and trends.

Competitor Analysis: Analyze competitors' websites to identify keywords they are ranking for and use these insights to supplement your keyword list.

3. Types of Keywords:

Short-Tail Keywords: Broad and general terms (e.g., "digital marketing") with high search volumes but high competition.

Long-Tail Keywords: More specific and targeted phrases (e.g., "best digital marketing strategies for startups") with lower search volumes but lower competition and higher conversion potential.

4. Factors to Consider:

Search Volume: Determine the average number of searches a keyword receives per month to estimate its popularity.

Keyword Difficulty: Assess the competition level for each keyword, considering how hard it would be to rank for it.

Relevance and Intent: Ensure the keywords align with your content, products, or services and match the search intent of users.

5. Organizing and Prioritizing Keywords:

Keyword Grouping: Group related keywords together based on themes, topics, or intent.

Prioritization: Prioritize keywords based on relevance, search volume, competition, and your content/marketing goals.

6. Refinement and Optimization:

Long-Term Strategy: Continuously refine and update your keyword list based on changing trends, user behavior, and algorithm updates.

Content Optimization: Integrate chosen keywords naturally into your content, including titles, headings, body text, and meta tags, to improve visibility and relevance.

7. Analyzing Performance:

Monitor and Measure: Use analytics tools to track keyword performance, including rankings, traffic, and conversions.

Iterative Improvement: Adjust your strategy based on performance data, focusing on high-performing keywords and optimizing underperforming ones.

By conducting thorough keyword research, businesses can create content that matches user intent, improves search engine rankings, drives targeted traffic, and ultimately leads to higher engagement and conversions.

CONTENT STRUCTURE

Content structure refers to the organization, layout, and presentation of information within a piece of content. A well-structured content piece is essential for readability, user engagement, and search engine optimization. Here's a detailed explanation of content structure:

1. Define the Objective and Audience:

• Identify Goals: Determine the purpose of the content—whether it's to inform, entertain, educate, or persuade.

• Understand Audience: Define your target audience's demographics, interests, preferences, and pain points to tailor the content accordingly.

2. Research and Outline:

• Topic Research: Gather information, facts, and data relevant to the chosen topic.

• Create an Outline: Organize the information into a clear outline with sections, headings, and subheadings. Arrange main points and supporting details logically.

3. Introduction:

• Hook or Attention Grabber: Begin with a compelling introduction that grabs the reader's attention. It could be a question, an interesting fact, a story, or a statement that piques curiosity.

• Thesis or Main Point: Clearly state the main purpose or thesis of the content. Let readers know what they can expect and why the content is valuable to them.

4. Body Content:

• Hierarchy with Headings and Subheadings: Organize content using headings (H1, H2, H3, etc.) and subheadings to create a logical structure. Headings should convey the main points and subtopics.

• Sections and Paragraphs: Break content into sections and paragraphs. Each section should cover a specific aspect or idea related to the overall topic. Paragraphs should be concise, focused, and easy to read.

• Use of Bullets and Lists: When appropriate, use bulleted or numbered lists to emphasize key points or steps. Lists help improve readability and highlight important information.

• Visual Elements: Incorporate images, infographics, videos, or other visual aids to complement and enhance the text. Visuals break the monotony of text and help illustrate complex concepts.

5. Transitions and Flow:

• Logical Flow: Ensure a smooth transition between sections and paragraphs. Use transitional words and phrases to connect ideas and maintain a coherent flow throughout the content.

• Linking: Internal and external linking can add depth and credibility to your content. Link to relevant sources, other articles on your website, or authoritative external sites for additional information.

6. Conclusion:

• Summarize Key Points: Recap the main points discussed in the content. Reinforce the thesis statement or main message.

• Call to Action (CTA): Encourage readers to take the next step — whether it's subscribing to a newsletter, contacting your business, or exploring related content.

7. Editing and Revision:

• Proofread for Clarity: Review the content for grammar, spelling, and punctuation errors.

• Readability Check: Ensure sentences and paragraphs flow smoothly and are easily understandable.

• Structural Review: Verify that the content adheres to the outlined structure, and adjust as needed for coherence and consistency.

8. Optimization and Formatting:

• SEO Optimization: Incorporate relevant keywords naturally within the content while adhering to SEO best practices.

• Formatting: Use formatting elements such as bullet points, numbered lists, bold text, and italics to highlight key information and improve readability.

9. Review and Feedback:

• Seek Feedback: Share the content with peers or colleagues for constructive feedback.

• Incorporate Suggestions: Consider and integrate valuable feedback to enhance the content structure and quality.

10. Finalize and Publish:

• Final Checks: Conduct a final review to ensure all elements are in place and the content meets the intended objectives and audience needs.

• Publish and Promote: Publish the content across relevant platforms and channels. Share it on social media, email newsletters, or other distribution channels to reach your audience.

Importance of Content Structure:

• Readability and User Experience: A well-structured content piece is easy to read and understand, improving user experience and engagement.

• SEO-Friendly: Search engines favor well-organized content. Proper headings, subheadings, and a clear structure help search engines understand the content's context and relevance.

• Information Accessibility: A clear structure makes information more accessible, allowing readers to quickly find what they're looking for.

• Skimmable Content: Structured content with headings and bullet points facilitates skimming, enabling readers to grasp the main points without reading every word.

• Improved Retention and Engagement: Structured content enhances reader retention by presenting information in a logical sequence, keeping readers engaged throughout.

Creating a strong content structure involves careful planning, organization, and consideration of the target audience's preferences and needs. It's essential for delivering valuable and easily digestible content that effectively communicates your message.

Content optimization involves various techniques aimed at improving a piece of content's visibility, relevance, and user experience. Here's a detailed explanation of optimization techniques:

1. Keyword Optimization:

• Keyword Research: Identify relevant keywords aligned with your content's topic and audience intent.

• Strategic Placement: Place keywords naturally in the title, headings, subheadings, URL, meta descriptions, and throughout the content.

• Avoid Keyword Stuffing: Ensure keywords are used in a way that sounds natural and doesn't compromise readability.

2. Content Quality and Relevance:

• Valuable and Engaging Content: Provide informative, valuable, and well-researched content that meets user needs.

• Content-Length: Create comprehensive content when appropriate, as longer, in-depth articles tend to perform well in search results.

• Useful Multimedia: Incorporate relevant images, videos, infographics, or other multimedia to enhance content quality and engagement.

3. User Experience (UX) Optimization:

• Mobile-Friendliness: Ensure your content is optimized for mobile devices as mobile compatibility is crucial for user experience and SEO.

• Page Load Speed: Optimize page speed to enhance user experience, as faster-loading pages tend to rank higher.

4. On-Page SEO:

• Meta Tags: Craft compelling meta titles and descriptions using relevant keywords to encourage clicks from search engine results pages (SERPs).

• Structured Data Markup: Implement structured data (schema markup) to help search engines better understand and display your content in rich snippets.

• Internal Linking: Link relevant pages within your website to guide users to additional valuable content and improve website navigation.

5. Off-Page SEO:

- Backlinks: Acquire high-quality backlinks from reputable and relevant websites to improve authority and trustworthiness.

- Social Signals: Encourage social sharing and engagement to indirectly impact search engine rankings.

6. Technical SEO:

- Crawlability and Indexing: Ensure search engines can easily crawl and index your content by using a proper sitemap and robots.txt file.

- HTTPS Security: Secure your website with HTTPS encryption to improve trust and ranking.

7. Content Formatting:

- Readable Structure: Use clear headings, subheadings, bullet points, and paragraphs to enhance readability.

- Rich Snippets: Utilize featured snippets or rich results by formatting content in ways search engines understand for enhanced visibility.

8. Regular Updates and Maintenance:

- Freshness: Update content regularly to keep it relevant and accurate, which can positively impact search rankings.

• Fix Broken Links and Errors: Regularly check and fix broken links, 404 errors, and other technical issues to maintain a good user experience.

9. Analyze and Optimize:

• Monitor Performance: Use analytics tools to track content performance, understand user behavior, and adjust strategies accordingly.

• Iterative Improvement: Continuously optimize based on data insights, user feedback, and evolving SEO trends to refine your content strategy.

10. Accessibility and Compliance:

• Accessibility Standards: Ensure your content complies with web accessibility standards to cater to all users, including those with disabilities.

Optimization is an ongoing process that involves a combination of technical enhancements, content quality improvements, and user-centric strategies. Implementing these techniques can significantly improve a piece of content's visibility, relevance, and overall impact on search engine rankings and user engagement.

TIPS ON STORYTELLING, SEO BEST PRACTICES, AND MAINTAINING CONSISTENCY.

Here are tips for storytelling, SEO best practices, and maintaining consistency in your content creation:

Storytelling Tips:

• Know Your Audience: Understand your audience's interests, preferences, and pain points. Tailor your story to resonate with their emotions and experiences.

• Create a Compelling Narrative: Develop a narrative arc that includes a beginning (setting the scene), a middle (conflict or challenge), and an end (resolution or outcome).

• Focus on Emotion: Use storytelling to evoke emotions. Emotionally resonant stories are more memorable and impactful.

• Use Concrete Examples: Incorporate specific and relatable examples or anecdotes to illustrate your message effectively.

• Character Development: Introduce characters (even if they are representations of real situations or personas) to create relatable connections with your audience.

• Keep it Authentic: Be genuine and authentic in your storytelling. Authenticity builds trust and credibility with your audience.

SEO Best Practices:

• Keyword Research and Integration: Conduct thorough keyword research to identify relevant terms. Integrate keywords naturally within your content while maintaining readability.

• High-Quality Content: Create valuable, informative, and engaging content. High-quality content tends to perform better in search rankings.

• Optimize Titles and Meta Descriptions: Craft compelling titles and meta descriptions using relevant keywords to improve click-through rates in search results.

• Optimize for Mobile: Ensure your website and content are mobile-friendly, as mobile optimization is crucial for SEO.

• Site Structure and Internal Linking: Organize your site's structure logically and employ internal linking to improve navigation and user experience.

• Optimize for Speed: Improve page loading speed as faster sites tend to rank higher. Compress images, use caching, and optimize code for better performance.

Maintaining Consistency:

• Create a Content Calendar: Plan and schedule content in advance using a content calendar. Maintain consistency in posting schedules to keep your audience engaged.

• Define Brand Voice and Style: Establish a consistent brand voice, tone, and style across all content. Consistency builds brand identity and recognition.

• Stick to Themes and Topics: Maintain consistency by focusing on specific themes or topics that align with your brand and resonate with your audience.

• Engage with Your Audience: Encourage interaction, respond to comments, and seek feedback. Engaging with your audience regularly helps in building relationships.

• Review and Refine: Regularly review content performance metrics. Analyze what works and what doesn't, then refine your strategies accordingly.

• Document Guidelines: Create style guides or content guidelines to ensure consistency in formatting, tone, and messaging.

By implementing these tips, you can craft compelling stories, optimize your content for search engines, and maintain consistency in your content creation efforts, thereby enhancing engagement and driving better results for your brand.

THE VARIOUS CONTENT DISTRIBUTION CHANNELS

Content distribution channels are platforms or mediums through which content is shared, promoted, and disseminated to reach a target audience. Here's an in-depth discussion of various content distribution channels:

Owned Channels:

• Website/Blog: A central hub for content, offering versatility to publish different content types like articles, videos, infographics, etc. It's under your control and ideal for SEO.

• Email Newsletters: Direct communication with subscribers, providing personalized and targeted content updates, promotions, or information.

• Social Media Profiles: Utilize platforms like Facebook, Twitter, LinkedIn, Instagram, and others to share content, engage with followers, and build a community.

• Mobile Apps: If applicable, mobile apps allow direct access to your content, fostering user engagement and loyalty.

Earned Channels:

• Press and Media Coverage: Gain exposure through media outlets, news articles, or interviews. Earned media boosts credibility and visibility.

• Influencer Marketing: Collaborate with influencers who resonate with your audience to reach their followers authentically.

• User-Generated Content (UGC): Encourage your audience to create and share content related to your brand, products, or services. UGC boosts authenticity and engagement.

• Word-of-Mouth and Referrals: Satisfied customers referring your brand or content to others can be a powerful form of earned distribution.

Paid Channels:

• Paid Advertising: Utilize platforms like Google Ads, social media ads, native advertising, or display ads to reach specific audiences and promote content.

• Sponsored Content: Paying for content placement on third-party websites or publications to gain visibility and reach new audiences.

• Content Syndication: Distribute content to other websites or platforms for a fee to extend reach beyond your owned channels.

Offline Channels:

• Print Media: Magazines, newspapers, brochures, and other printed materials can still be effective in reaching certain demographics or local audiences.

• Events and Conferences: Speaking engagements, trade shows, or sponsoring events can showcase your expertise and connect directly with audiences.

• Direct Mail: Sending physical promotional materials or catalogs through mail to targeted recipients.

Emerging Channels:

• Podcasts: Audio-based content platforms where you can share knowledge, interviews, stories, etc., reaching audiences interested in auditory content.

• Live Streaming: Platforms like Twitch, YouTube Live, or Facebook Live offer real-time content delivery, fostering engagement and interaction.

• Voice Search and AI Assistants: Optimize content for voice search queries as voice assistants become more prevalent in search.

• VR/AR Platforms: Explore virtual or augmented reality platforms for immersive storytelling or product experiences.

Factors to Consider When Choosing Channels:

• Audience Preferences: Understand where your target audience spends their time and tailor content distribution accordingly.

• Content Format: Certain channels may be more conducive to specific content types (e.g., visual content on Instagram, long-form articles on a blog).

• Goals and Budget: Consider your content marketing goals and allocate resources effectively to the channels that align with those objectives.

• Analytics and Insights: Continuously monitor performance metrics to assess which channels drive the most engagement, conversions, or ROI.

Selecting the right mix of distribution channels based on your content strategy, audience preferences, and goals is crucial for effectively reaching and engaging your target audience. Regularly assess and adapt your distribution strategy to optimize performance and maximize the impact of your content.

HOW TO LEVERAGE THE VARIOUS CONTENT DISTRIBUTION CHANNELS EFFECTIVELY

Leveraging content distribution channels effectively involves strategic planning, content optimization, and audience targeting. Here's a guide on how to make the most of different distribution channels:

1. Understand Your Audience:

Audience Segmentation: Segment your audience based on demographics, interests, behavior, and preferences.

Channel Preferences: Identify which channels your target audience frequents and prefers for consuming content.

2. Tailor Content for Each Channel:

Adapt Content Format: Customize content formats (videos, articles, infographics, etc.) based on the channel's requirements and audience preferences.

Optimize for Platform: Adjust content length, tone, and style to suit the specific platform's norms and user expectations.

3. Create a Content Distribution Strategy:

Channel Selection: Choose channels that align with your content and audience. Prioritize those that deliver the best results based on analytics.

Consistent Branding: Maintain a consistent brand voice, style, and messaging across all channels for brand recognition and coherence.

4. Optimize SEO for Content Distribution:

Keyword Optimization: Use relevant keywords in content titles, descriptions, and captions to enhance discoverability across search engines and platforms.

Link Building: Foster backlinks by sharing content on multiple platforms and encouraging others to link back to your content.

5. Engage and Interact:

Active Participation: Engage with your audience through comments, replies, and conversations. Foster discussions and respond to feedback.

Community Building: Create communities around your content by encouraging user-generated content, sharing user stories, and running contests or polls.

6. Measure and Analyze Performance:

Track Metrics: Use analytics tools to measure the performance of each distribution channel. Analyze metrics such as engagement, click-through rates, conversions, and audience demographics.

Iterative Improvement: Based on data insights, refine your content strategy. Focus more on channels that deliver better results and tweak strategies for underperforming ones.

7. Experiment and Innovate:

A/B Testing: Experiment with different content formats, posting times, or messaging strategies to understand what resonates best with your audience.

Explore New Channels: Stay updated with emerging platforms and technologies. Experiment with new channels to diversify your content distribution strategy.

8. Create Consistency Across Channels:

Content Calendar: Maintain a consistent posting schedule across channels. Plan content in advance using a content calendar to ensure regular and timely updates.

Cross-Promotion: Promote content across multiple channels to increase visibility and reach a wider audience.

9. Leverage Paid Advertising:

Targeted Ads: Utilize paid advertising options available on various platforms to reach specific audience segments effectively.

Sponsored Content: Invest in sponsored content or native advertising opportunities on platforms where your audience spends time.

10. Monitor Trends and Adapt:

Stay Updated: Keep an eye on industry trends, changes in algorithms, and new features on platforms. Adapt your strategies accordingly to stay relevant.

By leveraging content distribution channels effectively, you can maximize your content's reach, engagement, and impact on your target audience. Regularly assess performance, adapt strategies, and experiment with new tactics to optimize your content distribution efforts.

HOW TO DEVELOP A CONTENT DISTRIBUTION STRATEGY

Developing a content distribution strategy involves planning and outlining the approach to disseminate content effectively across various channels to reach and engage your target audience. Here's a step-by-step guide to creating a content distribution strategy:

1. Define Goals and Objectives:

Identify Goals: Determine what you want to achieve with your content distribution — whether it's brand awareness, lead generation, increased website traffic, or sales.

Set Measurable Objectives: Establish clear, quantifiable objectives that align with your goals. For example, aim for a specific increase in website traffic or engagement metrics.

2. Understand Your Audience:

Audience Analysis: Conduct thorough research to understand your target audience's demographics, behaviors, preferences, interests, and pain points.

Channel Preferences: Identify the channels and platforms your audience frequents to consume content — social media, blogs, forums, etc.

3. Audit Existing Content and Assets:

Content Inventory: Assess your existing content assets — blog posts, videos, infographics, etc. Identify high-performing content that can be repurposed or optimized for distribution.

Content Gap Analysis: Identify topics or formats missing from your current content library that could fill gaps in your audience's needs.

4. Choose Relevant Distribution Channels:

Channel Selection: Based on audience preferences and your content types, choose channels that align with your objectives. Consider owned, earned, and paid channels.

Prioritize Channels: Prioritize channels based on their effectiveness in reaching your target audience and achieving your goals.

5. Define Content Types and Formats:

Content Formats: Determine which content formats (articles, videos, podcasts, infographics, etc.) work best for each channel and audience segment.

Adaptation and Repurposing: Plan how content can be adapted or repurposed across different channels without compromising quality or relevance.

6. Create a Content Calendar:

Schedule Content: Develop a content calendar outlining when and where content will be published on each channel. Ensure consistency in posting schedules.

Content Themes and Topics: Define content themes and topics aligned with your audience's interests and preferences. Map these to your content calendar.

7. Establish Distribution Tactics:

Social Media Distribution: Plan social media posts, considering optimal times for engagement and the type of content each platform favors.

Email Marketing: Develop an email distribution plan for newsletters, updates, or targeted campaigns to segmented subscriber lists.

Paid Promotion: Consider allocating budget for paid promotion or advertising to boost content visibility on selected platforms.

8. Implement and Monitor:

Execute the Plan: Start distributing content across chosen channels according to the content calendar.

Measure Performance: Use analytics tools to track the performance of each distribution channel. Monitor metrics such as engagement, traffic, conversions, and audience demographics.

9. Analyze, Optimize, and Adapt:

Assess Results: Analyze the performance data to determine which channels and content types are most effective in achieving your goals.

Optimization: Based on insights, optimize your distribution strategy by tweaking content formats, posting times, or channel selection.

10. Iterate and Evolve:

Continuous Improvement: Regularly review and refine your content distribution strategy based on changing audience behaviors, industry trends, and performance data.

Experimentation: Test new tactics or channels and assess their impact. Be willing to adapt and evolve your strategy based on experimentation results.

Developing a content distribution strategy requires a holistic approach, understanding your audience, aligning with business goals, and continuous monitoring and optimization. It's an iterative process that evolves over time to effectively deliver content to the right audience, in the right format, and at the right time.

STRATEGIES FOR PROMOTING CONTENT ACROSS DIFFERENT PLATFORMS

Promoting content across various platforms requires tailored strategies that consider the unique characteristics and audience behavior of each platform. Here are strategies for promoting content across different platforms:

Social Media Platforms:

• Platform-Specific Content: Customize content for each platform. Use visually appealing images on Instagram, concise messages on Twitter, and longer-form content on LinkedIn or Facebook.

• Engagement and Interaction: Engage with your audience by responding to comments, initiating discussions, and sharing user-generated content to foster community engagement.

• Utilize Stories and Live Video: Leverage features like Stories on Instagram/Facebook or live video streaming to provide real-time updates or behind-the-scenes content.

• Hashtags and Tagging: Use relevant hashtags to expand reach and increase discoverability. Tag relevant users, brands, or influencers to encourage shares and interactions.

Email Marketing:

• Segmented Campaigns: Personalize email campaigns by segmenting your audience based on interests, behavior, or demographics. Deliver targeted content relevant to each segment.

• Compelling Subject Lines: Craft engaging subject lines that encourage recipients to open and read your emails.

• Call-to-Action (CTA): Include clear and compelling CTAs to prompt readers to take desired actions, such as visiting your website, downloading content, or making a purchase.

Blog and Content Platforms:

• Guest Blogging: Collaborate with influencers or industry experts for guest posts on their blogs. This can expand your reach to their audience and build credibility.

• Cross-Linking: Link internally within your blog or content platform to guide readers to related or relevant content, improving engagement and time spent on your site.

• Promotion within Content: Incorporate links to your other content pieces, products, or services naturally within your blog posts or articles.

Video-Sharing Platforms:

• Optimized Video Content: Create visually appealing, engaging videos tailored to the platform's audience and preferences (e.g., short, engaging videos for TikTok, longer tutorials for YouTube).

• Engagement Features: Encourage comments, likes, shares, and subscriptions by asking questions, prompting discussions, or running contests related to your videos.

• Collaborations and Influencer Partnerships: Partner with influencers or collaborate with other content creators to reach their audience and expand your video's visibility.

Paid Advertising Platforms:

• Targeted Ads: Utilize targeting options provided by advertising platforms (e.g., Google Ads, Facebook Ads) to reach specific demographics, interests, or behaviors.

• A/B Testing: Experiment with different ad creatives, headlines, or targeting parameters to optimize ad performance and maximize ROI.

• Retargeting Campaigns: Implement retargeting ads to re-engage users who have previously interacted with your content or visited your website.

Community and Forum Platforms:

• **Engage Authentically:** Participate in relevant communities or forums by providing valuable insights, answering questions, and offering solutions without overtly promoting your content.

• **Signature Links:** Use forum signatures or profiles to include links to your content or website discreetly within your contributions.

• **Community Guidelines Compliance:** Respect community rules and guidelines by contributing meaningfully without spamming or self-promotion.

Influencer and Partnership Collaborations:

• **Influencer Marketing:** Partner with influencers or industry leaders to promote your content to their followers authentically.

• **Co-Creation:** Collaborate with influencers or partners to co-create content (e.g., webinars, podcasts, or joint campaigns) that mutually benefits both parties and resonates with their audience.

• **Affiliate Marketing:** Explore affiliate partnerships where influencers or partners promote your content in exchange for a commission or other benefits.

When promoting content across different platforms, it's crucial to adapt your strategies to suit each platform's audience and dynamics. Consistency, authenticity, and value delivery should remain at the core of your promotional efforts across all platforms.

THE IMPORTANCE OF REPURPOSING CONTENT FOR DIFFERENT CHANNELS

Repurposing content for different channels is crucial in maximizing the value and reach of your content. Here's why repurposing content holds immense importance:

1. Expanding Reach and Audience:

Targeting Diverse Audiences: Different channels attract distinct demographics and preferences. Repurposing content allows you to tailor the same message to various audience segments.

Reaching Non-Traditional Audiences: Not all audiences consume content in the same format or on the same platforms. Repurposing content ensures that your message reaches those who prefer different mediums.

2. Improved Visibility and Engagement:

Increased Exposure: Repurposing allows you to distribute content across multiple channels, increasing its visibility and chances of being discovered by a wider audience.

Enhanced Engagement: Different formats resonate differently with audiences. By repurposing content into various formats (e.g., video, infographics, blog posts), you can engage audiences who prefer visual, textual, or audio content.

3. Cost and Time Efficiency:

Maximizing Content Investment: Repurposing extracts more value from existing content assets without requiring substantial additional resources or creation from scratch.

Time-Saving: Adapting existing content to different formats or channels typically takes less time than producing entirely new content, enabling a faster content publishing cycle.

4. Reinforcing Brand Messaging:

Consistent Branding: Repurposing content ensures that your core message and brand values remain consistent across various channels, reinforcing brand identity and recognition.

Increased Memorability: Consistent messaging across different formats reinforces key points, making them more memorable for the audience.

5. SEO Benefits:

Improved Search Rankings: Repurposing content in different formats and distributing it across multiple platforms can improve your online presence and search engine rankings.

Backlink Opportunities: Different content formats may attract different types of backlinks, contributing to a diverse and robust link profile.

6. Adapting to Audience Preferences:

Catering to Preferences: Some audiences prefer visual content (videos, infographics), while others prefer written content (blogs, articles). Repurposing allows you to accommodate diverse audience preferences.

Meeting Platform Requirements: Each platform has its own specifications and limitations. Adapting content ensures it fits seamlessly into each platform's requirements without compromising quality.

7. Longevity and Evergreen Content:

Breathing New Life: Repurposing allows you to refresh older content by presenting it in a new format or context, extending its lifespan and relevance.

Leveraging Evergreen Content: Evergreen content can be repurposed regularly without losing its value, providing timeless information to new audiences.

In summary, repurposing content for different channels allows you to maximize its impact, reach, and longevity, catering to diverse audience preferences while optimizing resources and efforts in content creation and distribution.

PAID PROMOTION AND ORGANIC REACH TACTICS

Paid promotion and organic reach tactics are essential components of a comprehensive content distribution strategy. Here's a breakdown of each and insights on how to leverage them effectively:

Paid Promotion:

1. Targeted Advertising:

Platforms: Utilize paid advertising options on platforms like Google Ads, Facebook Ads, LinkedIn Ads, or Twitter Ads to reach specific demographics, interests, or behaviors.

Targeting: Use advanced targeting features to reach a highly segmented audience based on factors such as age, location, interests, and online behavior.

Budget Allocation: Set budgets and bidding strategies aligned with your goals, adjusting based on performance metrics.

2. Sponsored Content:

Native Advertising: Invest in sponsored content placements on third-party websites or publications that align with your audience's interests.

Influencer Collaborations: Partner with influencers or industry experts for sponsored posts to tap into their engaged audience.

3. Retargeting Campaigns:

Remarketing: Implement retargeting ads to re-engage users who have previously interacted with your content or visited your website.

Customized Messaging: Tailor retargeting ads based on users' previous interactions to encourage conversions.

4. A/B Testing:

Experimentation: Test different ad creatives, headlines, targeting parameters, or call-to-actions to optimize ad performance.

Data-Driven Decisions: Analyze A/B test results and iterate to improve ad effectiveness and ROI.

Organic Reach Tactics:

1. High-Quality Content Creation:

Valuable Content: Produce high-quality, valuable content that resonates with your audience, encourages shares, and attracts organic engagement.

Consistency: Regularly publish relevant and engaging content to keep your audience engaged and coming back for more.

2. Search Engine Optimization (SEO):

Keyword Optimization: Optimize content using relevant keywords to improve organic search rankings and increase visibility.

On-Page and Off-Page SEO: Focus on both on-page elements (meta tags, content structure) and off-page factors (backlinks, site authority).

3. Social Media Engagement:

Community Building: Foster a community around your brand by engaging with your audience, encouraging discussions, and responding promptly.

User-Generated Content: Encourage user-generated content, which can amplify organic reach and authenticity.

4. Influencer Partnerships:

Authentic Collaborations: Partner with influencers whose audience aligns with yours for authentic promotions and to reach a wider, engaged audience.

Co-Creation: Collaborate with influencers on content creation or campaigns for mutual benefit.

5. Email Marketing and Newsletters:

Segmentation: Segment your email lists to provide personalized and relevant content to different audience segments.

Compelling Subject Lines and Content: Craft enticing subject lines and valuable content to increase open rates and engagement.

6. Content Distribution Strategy:

Multichannel Approach: Distribute content strategically across various platforms to maximize organic visibility and engagement.

Consistent Branding: Maintain consistent branding and messaging across all platforms to reinforce brand identity.

Balancing paid promotion tactics with organic reach strategies is crucial for a well-rounded content distribution approach. By leveraging both effectively, you can extend your content's reach, engage your audience, and achieve your content marketing goals.

CHAPTER FOUR

KEY METRICS TO MEASURE CONTENT MARKETING SUCCESS

Measuring the success of your content marketing efforts involves tracking various key performance indicators (KPIs) that align with your goals and objectives. Here are key metrics to consider for measuring content marketing success:

1. Website Traffic Metrics:

• Page Views: Total number of pages viewed on your website, indicating overall traffic volume.

• Unique Visitors: Number of distinct individuals visiting your site, providing insights into your audience reach.

• Bounce Rate: Percentage of visitors who leave your site after viewing only one page, reflecting engagement and content relevancy.

• Time on Page: Average time visitors spend on your site, indicating content engagement levels.

2. Engagement Metrics:

• Social Media Engagement: Likes, shares, comments, and clicks on social media platforms, showcasing audience interaction with your content.

• Comments and Replies: Number of comments and responses on your blog posts or articles, indicating audience engagement and interest.

• Email Metrics: Open rates, click-through rates, and conversion rates from email campaigns, measuring audience response to your content.

3. Conversion and Lead Metrics:

• Conversion Rate: Percentage of visitors who complete a desired action (e.g., sign-ups, downloads, purchases), indicating content effectiveness in driving conversions.

• Lead Generation: Number of leads generated through content, such as form submissions, inquiries, or registrations.

• Sales Attribution: Measure content's impact on sales and revenue generation through attribution models.

4. SEO and Search Metrics:

• Keyword Rankings: Monitor rankings for targeted keywords on search engines to gauge SEO effectiveness.

• Organic Traffic: Measure traffic originating from organic search, showcasing content's visibility and search engine performance.

• Backlinks: Track the number and quality of backlinks to your content, which influences search engine rankings.

5. Content Performance Metrics:

• Content Engagement: Analyze specific content performance, such as views, shares, time spent, and interaction rates.

• Top-performing Content: Identify high-performing content by assessing metrics like traffic, engagement, and conversion rates.

6. Customer Behavior and Retention Metrics:

• Customer Lifetime Value (CLV): Predicted revenue from a customer over the entire relationship, indicating the value of your content in customer retention and loyalty.

• Churn Rate: Percentage of customers who stop using your product or service, providing insights into content's impact on customer retention.

7. Cost and ROI Metrics:

• Cost per Acquisition (CPA): Cost incurred to acquire a new customer through content marketing efforts.

• Return on Investment (ROI): Measure the financial return relative to the cost of content marketing campaigns.

8. Audience Insights:

• Audience Demographics: Understand the characteristics of your audience, aiding in content personalization and targeting.

• Behavioral Insights: Analyze audience behavior patterns to optimize content strategies and distribution channels.

Selecting relevant metrics aligned with your content marketing goals and regularly analyzing these metrics is crucial in evaluating the success of your content strategy and making data-driven decisions for optimization and improvement.

HOW TO TRACK AND MEASURE CONTENT MARKETING METRICS

Tracking and measuring content marketing metrics involves a systematic approach to gather data, analyze performance, and derive actionable insights. Here's a step-by-step guide on how to track and measure content marketing metrics effectively:

1. Define Clear Objectives and Goals:

Identify Goals: Determine specific and measurable goals aligned with your content marketing strategy (e.g., increased brand awareness, lead generation, sales, etc.).

Establish KPIs: Define key performance indicators (KPIs) that directly relate to your goals and objectives.

2. Identify Relevant Metrics:

Choose Appropriate Metrics: Select metrics that align with your goals. Examples include website traffic, engagement rates, conversions, SEO performance, etc.

Prioritize Key Metrics: Focus on a few critical metrics rather than tracking too many, ensuring they directly impact your goals.

3. Implement Analytics Tools:

Use Analytics Platforms: Utilize tools like Google Analytics, social media analytics, email marketing platforms (e.g., Mailchimp), and CRM systems to track and gather data.

Set Up Tracking Parameters: Implement UTM parameters for tracking URLs, enabling better analysis of traffic sources and campaign performance.

4. Track Website and Traffic Metrics:

Website Traffic: Monitor metrics like total visits, unique visitors, page views, bounce rate, and average session duration using Google Analytics or similar tools.

Conversion Tracking: Set up conversion tracking to measure specific actions users take on your site, such as form submissions, downloads, or purchases.

5. Analyze Engagement Metrics:

Social Media Engagement: Track likes, shares, comments, and clicks on social media platforms to gauge audience interaction and content performance.

Email Metrics: Monitor email open rates, click-through rates (CTRs), and conversion rates from email campaigns to assess audience engagement.

6. Assess SEO and Search Metrics:

Keyword Rankings: Monitor keyword positions in search engine results pages (SERPs) using tools like SEMrush or Moz to evaluate SEO performance.

Organic Traffic: Analyze organic traffic data to measure the volume and quality of traffic originating from search engines.

7. Evaluate Content Performance:

Content Engagement: Review specific content performance metrics such as views, shares, time spent, and interaction rates for individual pieces of content.

Identify Top-Performing Content: Identify high-performing content based on traffic, engagement, and conversion metrics to replicate success.

8. Measure Conversion and ROI Metrics:

Conversion Rate: Calculate conversion rates for different content campaigns to determine their effectiveness in driving desired actions.

Return on Investment (ROI): Assess the financial return relative to the cost of content marketing efforts to evaluate campaign success.

9. Regularly Analyze and Report:

Create Custom Reports: Generate customized reports using analytics tools to visualize data and trends for better insights.

Regular Review: Regularly review and analyze metrics to understand performance, identify trends, and make data-driven decisions for optimization.

10. Iterate and Optimize:

Iterative Improvement: Use insights gained from metrics to refine content strategies, optimize campaigns, and improve performance continuously.

A/B Testing: Conduct experiments and A/B tests based on data insights to refine content, distribution methods, and audience targeting.

By following these steps and consistently monitoring and analyzing content marketing metrics, you can gain valuable insights into the performance of your content efforts, make informed decisions, and continually improve your content strategy for better results.

HOW TO USE ANALYTICS TOOLS TO TRACK PERFORMANCE

Analytics tools are essential for tracking and analyzing performance metrics in content marketing. Here's a detailed guide on using analytics tools to track and measure content performance:

1. Setting Up Analytics Tools:

- Google Analytics:

Account Setup: Create a Google Analytics account and install the tracking code on your website.

Goal Configuration: Define goals (e.g., form submissions, purchases) to track specific actions on your site.

- Social Media Analytics:

Platform Insights: Use native analytics tools provided by social media platforms (Facebook Insights, Twitter Analytics, LinkedIn Analytics) to access data on engagement, audience demographics, and content performance.

- Email Marketing Platforms:

Tracking Codes: Implement tracking codes or pixels provided by email marketing platforms to monitor email open rates, click-through rates, and conversion rates.

2. Tracking Website and Traffic Metrics:

- Sessions and Users: Monitor the number of sessions (visits) and unique users accessing your website over a specific period.

- Page Views: Track the total number of pages viewed by visitors to understand content consumption patterns.

• Bounce Rate: Measure the percentage of single-page visits, indicating the proportion of visitors who left without interacting further.

3. Analyzing Engagement Metrics:

• Social Media Engagement: Assess likes, shares, comments, and clicks on social media posts to gauge audience interaction and content performance.

• Email Engagement: Analyze email open rates, click-through rates (CTRs), and conversion rates to understand audience engagement with email content.

4. Evaluating SEO and Search Metrics:

• Keyword Rankings: Use tools like SEMrush, Moz, or Ahrefs to track keyword rankings and identify opportunities for improving search visibility.

• Organic Traffic: Analyze organic traffic data in Google Analytics to measure traffic volume and sources from search engines.

5. Assessing Content Performance:

• Content Engagement: Review individual content performance metrics like views, shares, time spent, and interaction rates across different channels.

• Identify Top-Performing Content: Identify high-performing content based on traffic, engagement, and conversion metrics to replicate success.

6. Measuring Conversion and ROI Metrics:

• Conversion Tracking: Monitor conversions such as form submissions, downloads, or purchases attributed to specific content or campaigns.

• Return on Investment (ROI): Calculate the ROI by comparing the cost of content creation and distribution to the resulting revenue or leads generated.

7. Customizing Reports and Dashboards:

• Custom Reports: Create custom reports in Google Analytics or other analytics tools to visualize and analyze data specific to your content marketing goals.

• Dashboards: Build dashboards with key metrics to have a quick overview of content performance across channels.

8. Iterative Improvement and Optimization:

• Data Analysis: Regularly analyze performance metrics to identify trends, patterns, and areas for improvement.

• Optimization Strategies: Use insights gained from analytics to refine content strategies, distribution methods, and audience targeting for better results.

9. Experimentation and A/B Testing:

• Testing Hypotheses: Conduct A/B tests based on data insights to compare variations in content, headlines, visuals, or distribution channels.

• Evaluate Results: Analyze A/B test results to make data-driven decisions and optimize content strategies based on what works best.

10. Training and Learning:

• Stay Updated: Keep learning about new features, updates, and best practices for using analytics tools through training courses, webinars, or tutorials offered by these platforms.

• Continuous Improvement: Regularly seek opportunities to enhance your analytics skills to extract more valuable insights from the data.

By utilizing these steps and practices, marketers can effectively use analytics tools to track, measure, and analyze content performance across various channels, enabling data-driven decision-making and continual optimization of content marketing strategies.

THE IMPORTANCE OF ANALYZING DATA AND MAKING ADJUSTMENTS BASED ON INSIGHTS

Analyzing data and making adjustments based on insights are crucial aspects of any successful content marketing strategy. Here's why it's essential:

1. Data-Driven Decision Making:

Evidence-Based Insights: Data analysis provides concrete evidence of what works and what doesn't in your content marketing efforts.

Eliminates Guesswork: Rather than relying on assumptions, data allows you to make informed decisions backed by real metrics and audience behavior.

2. Continuous Improvement:

Optimization Opportunities: Analysis helps identify areas of improvement in content performance, distribution channels, or audience engagement.

Iterative Approach: Regular adjustments based on data insights facilitate ongoing refinement of strategies for better results.

3. Audience Understanding and Personalization:

Audience Insights: Data analysis offers deeper insights into audience preferences, behaviors, and needs.

Content Personalization: Adjustments based on these insights enable tailoring content to better resonate with specific audience segments, enhancing relevance and engagement.

4. Maximizing ROI and Resource Allocation:

Optimizing Investments: Data-driven adjustments help allocate resources more effectively by focusing efforts on high-performing content types, channels, or campaigns.

ROI Improvement: Identifying and eliminating underperforming strategies or content ensures better returns on investment.

5. Adapting to Trends and Changes:

Stay Relevant: Data analysis helps in staying abreast of changing trends, shifts in audience preferences, or alterations in search engine algorithms.

Adaptation Strategies: Adjustments based on insights allow adaptation to evolving market conditions, keeping your content strategy relevant.

6. Testing and Experimentation:

A/B Testing: Data analysis guides A/B testing initiatives, enabling the comparison of different content variations or strategies to determine the most effective approach.

Informed Experiments: Insights obtained from data aid in designing experiments and tests, leading to more impactful outcomes.

7. Enhancing Content Performance:

Improving Engagement: Adjustments based on data insights can enhance content quality, format, or distribution methods, leading to increased engagement and interaction.

Identifying Success Factors: Understanding what drives successful content helps replicate those elements in future strategies.

8. Goal Alignment and Accountability:

Goal Refinement: Regular analysis ensures that content marketing efforts remain aligned with overarching business goals.

Accountability and Measurement: Data analysis establishes clear metrics for measuring success, holding teams accountable for achieving objectives.

9. Agility and Flexibility:

Quick Response: Rapid adjustments based on real-time or near-real-time data enable agility in responding to changing market dynamics or audience demands.

Flexible Strategy: Insights allow for flexibility in modifying strategies, tactics, or campaigns as needed without rigid adherence to initial plans.

In summary, analyzing data and making adjustments based on insights empower marketers to refine strategies, optimize content, and adapt to changing market conditions. This iterative approach fosters continuous improvement and ensures that content marketing efforts remain effective, relevant, and aligned with business objectives.

HOW TO ANALYZE DATA AND MAKE DATA-DRIVEN DECISIONS

Analyzing data and making data-driven decisions in content marketing involves a systematic process to extract valuable insights from the collected data. Here's a detailed guide on how to analyze data and use it for informed decision-making:

1. Define Clear Objectives:

Establish Goals: Clearly define the objectives you aim to achieve through your content marketing efforts.

Identify Key Metrics: Determine the specific metrics and KPIs relevant to your goals.

2. Collect Relevant Data:

Utilize Analytics Tools: Gather data from various sources such as Google Analytics, social media insights, email marketing platforms, CRM systems, etc.

Structured Data Collection: Ensure consistent data collection methods to maintain data integrity and accuracy.

3. Data Cleaning and Preparation:

Data Quality Check: Verify data accuracy, completeness, and consistency to eliminate errors or discrepancies.

Data Formatting: Organize and structure data in a way that facilitates analysis and comparison.

4. Perform Data Analysis:

Descriptive Analysis: Summarize and describe collected data using techniques like averages, percentages, and visualizations (charts, graphs) for better comprehension.

Comparative Analysis: Compare different sets of data, such as performance across time periods, content types, or audience segments.

5. Identify Patterns and Trends:

Pattern Recognition: Look for recurring patterns or trends in the data that highlight successes, challenges, or changes in audience behavior.

Seasonal Trends: Identify any seasonal variations or cyclical patterns influencing content performance.

6. Interpret Insights and Draw Conclusions:

Contextualize Data: Understand the context behind the numbers to derive meaningful conclusions.

Cause-and-Effect Analysis: Connect data points to uncover cause-and-effect relationships influencing content performance.

7. Generate Actionable Insights:

Prioritize Findings: Focus on the most significant insights that directly impact your content marketing objectives.

Actionable Recommendations: Translate insights into actionable recommendations for strategy improvement.

8. Test Hypotheses and Strategies:

A/B Testing: Experiment with variations based on data insights to validate hypotheses or test different content strategies, formats, or distribution channels.

Pilot Tests: Run small-scale pilot tests for new strategies before implementing them on a larger scale.

9. Make Informed Decisions:

Data-Driven Decisions: Base decisions on the evidence and insights obtained from data analysis rather than assumptions or gut feelings.

Risk Assessment: Consider potential risks or uncertainties associated with decisions and weigh them against expected outcomes.

10. Implement Changes and Monitor Results:

Execute Adjustments: Implement changes or optimizations based on data-driven insights into content, distribution strategies, or audience targeting.

Continual Monitoring: Regularly monitor the impact of implemented changes and track new data to evaluate the effectiveness of decisions.

11. Document and Review:

Documentation: Keep records of data analysis processes, insights, decisions made, and their outcomes for future reference.

Periodic Review: Conduct periodic reviews to reassess strategies, analyze new data, and ensure continued alignment with objectives.

By following this systematic approach to data analysis and decision-making, content marketers can harness the power of data to optimize strategies, improve content performance, and drive meaningful results aligned with their goals.

TOOLS AND TECHNIqUES FOR ORGANIZING WORKFLOWS AND COLLABORATION

Organizing workflows and enabling collaboration is crucial for efficient content creation and management in content marketing. Here are tools and techniques to streamline workflows and enhance collaboration:

Project Management Tools:

• Asana: Enables task assignment, deadline setting, and progress tracking. Teams can organize content creation tasks, manage timelines, and collaborate effectively.

• Trello: Utilizes boards, lists, and cards for visual task management. It allows teams to organize content ideas, assign tasks, and track progress through different stages.

• Monday.com: Provides customizable workflow templates and visual project boards for managing content creation tasks, deadlines, and team collaboration.

• Basecamp: Offers centralized project management, including task assignment, file sharing, scheduling, and communication, facilitating team collaboration and organization.

Content Collaboration Platforms:

• Google Workspace (formerly G Suite): Provides tools like Google Drive, Docs, Sheets, and Slides for collaborative content creation, editing, and sharing among team members in real-time.

• Microsoft 365 (formerly Office 365): Offers collaborative features within Word, Excel, PowerPoint, and OneDrive, allowing multiple users to work on content simultaneously.

• Dropbox Paper: Combines document creation, collaboration, and task management, enabling teams to work on documents together while integrating with other Dropbox features.

• Notion: Acts as an all-in-one workspace for content planning, task management, and collaborative editing of documents, integrating wikis, databases, and project boards.

Communication and Messaging Tools:

• Slack: Facilitates real-time communication, file sharing, and team collaboration through channels, direct messages, and integrations with various apps and tools.

• Microsoft Teams: Combines messaging, video calls, file sharing, and collaboration tools within one platform, enabling seamless communication and project coordination.

• Zoom: Offers video conferencing, webinars, and screen sharing functionalities for remote team meetings, brainstorming sessions, and content planning discussions.

Content Version Control:

• GitHub: Primarily for developers but useful for version control and collaboration on content, allowing multiple contributors to work on content while tracking changes.

• GitLab: Similar to GitHub, providing version control, collaboration features, and a platform for managing and reviewing changes made to content.

Workflow Automation Tools:

• Zapier: Connects different apps and automates workflows, allowing seamless data transfer and automation of repetitive tasks, saving time and improving efficiency.

• Integromat: Offers automation and integration capabilities similar to Zapier, enabling users to create custom workflows and automate tasks across multiple apps.

Techniques for Effective Collaboration:

• Clear Communication: Establish communication guidelines, channels, and regular check-ins to ensure everyone is aligned and informed.

• Role Definitions: Clearly define roles and responsibilities within the team to avoid overlaps or gaps in tasks.

• Centralized Documentation: Maintain a centralized repository for guidelines, style sheets, and documentation to ensure consistency across content.

• Regular Reviews and Feedback: Encourage open feedback loops and conduct regular reviews to improve content quality and processes.

• Training and Onboarding: Provide training and onboarding sessions for new team members to familiarize them with tools and workflows.

By leveraging these tools and implementing effective collaboration techniques, content marketing teams can streamline workflows, enhance productivity, and foster seamless collaboration among team members, leading to more efficient content creation and management.

CHAPTER FIVE

COMMON PITFALLS IN CONTENT MARKETING AND HOW TO AVOID THEM.

Here are some common pitfalls in content marketing and strategies to avoid them:

1. Lack of Clear Strategy and Goals:

Pitfall: Absence of a defined content strategy and clear goals leads to unfocused efforts and haphazard content creation.

Avoidance Strategy: Develop a comprehensive content strategy aligned with business objectives. Define specific goals, target audience, content types, and distribution channels.

2. Inconsistent or Irregular Posting:

Pitfall: Irregular posting schedules or inconsistent content quality can result in reduced audience engagement and loss of interest.

Avoidance Strategy: Create a content calendar and adhere to a consistent posting schedule. Plan content in advance to maintain regularity and ensure high-quality, relevant content.

3. Ignoring Audience Needs and Preferences:

Pitfall: Failing to understand audience preferences, interests, and pain points leads to content that doesn't resonate with the target audience.

Avoidance Strategy: Conduct thorough audience research, create buyer personas, and tailor content to address audience needs. Continuously gather feedback and adjust content strategies accordingly.

4. Overlooking SEO and Optimization:

Pitfall: Neglecting SEO practices and content optimization limits visibility and hinders the content's discoverability on search engines.

Avoidance Strategy: Implement SEO best practices, conduct keyword research, optimize content for relevant keywords, use metadata effectively, and focus on user experience to improve search rankings.

5. Lack of Promotion and Distribution Strategy:

Pitfall: Creating great content but failing to promote it effectively results in limited reach and engagement.

Avoidance Strategy: Develop a comprehensive content distribution plan. Utilize various channels (social media, email, influencers) strategically to reach your target audience and amplify content reach.

6. Failure to Measure and Analyze Performance:

Pitfall: Neglecting to track and analyze key metrics leads to an inability to understand content effectiveness and make data-driven decisions.

Avoidance Strategy: Regularly monitor performance metrics (traffic, engagement, conversions) using analytics tools. Use insights to optimize content strategies and improve performance continually.

7. Not Adapting to Trends and Changes:

Pitfall: Sticking to outdated strategies or failing to adapt to industry trends leads to stagnation and reduced competitiveness.

Avoidance Strategy: Stay updated with industry trends, audience behaviors, and technological advancements. Adapt content strategies accordingly to remain relevant and competitive.

8. Lack of Experimentation and Innovation:

Pitfall: Avoiding experimentation and innovation limits creativity and prevents the discovery of new successful content approaches.

Avoidance Strategy: Encourage experimentation, A/B testing, and trying new content formats or distribution channels. Embrace innovation to keep content fresh and engaging.

9. Focusing Solely on Sales or Self-Promotion:

Pitfall: Overly promotional content without providing value or addressing audience needs can alienate audiences.

Avoidance Strategy: Prioritize providing value, educating, entertaining, and solving audience problems. Aim for a balanced mix of promotional and value-driven content.

10. Not Investing in Quality Content Creation:

Pitfall: Compromising on content quality, whether due to limited resources or rushed production, diminishes audience trust and engagement.

Avoidance Strategy: Allocate resources for quality content creation. Invest in skilled writers, designers, and tools to ensure content meets high standards and resonates with the audience.

By recognizing these pitfalls and implementing strategies to address them, content marketers can navigate challenges more effectively, enhance content effectiveness, and drive better results in their content marketing initiatives.

MISCONCEPTIONS OR INEFFECTIVE STRATEGIES THAT BEGINNERS SHOULD BE WARY OF

Here are some common misconceptions and ineffective strategies in content marketing that beginners should be wary of:

1. Quantity Over Quality:

Misconception: Believing that publishing a high volume of content is more important than focusing on quality.

Reality: Quality content that provides value and resonates with the audience is more impactful than a high quantity of mediocre content. Focus on relevance, value, and engagement rather than sheer volume.

2. Ignoring Audience Research:

Misconception: Assuming that creating content without understanding the audience's needs and preferences will still attract attention.

Reality: Audience research is critical. Ignoring audience interests and pain points leads to irrelevant content that fails to engage or resonate with the intended audience.

3. Overemphasis on Self-Promotion:

Misconception: Believing that content should solely promote products or services without offering value.

Reality: Content marketing is about building relationships and trust. Overly promotional content without providing educational or entertaining value can alienate audiences.

4. Neglecting SEO and Optimization:

Misconception: Thinking that great content will automatically rank high in search engines without SEO optimization.

Reality: SEO is crucial for content discoverability. Neglecting optimization practices like keyword research, meta tags, and mobile optimization can limit content visibility.

5. Lack of Consistency and Patience:

Misconception: Expecting immediate results and giving up quickly if content doesn't yield immediate success.

Reality: Content marketing is a long-term strategy. Consistency and patience are essential. It takes time to build an audience, gain visibility, and see measurable results.

6. Focusing Solely on Virality:

Misconception: Believing that creating viral content should be the primary goal of content marketing.

Reality: Viral content is unpredictable and doesn't guarantee sustained success. Focus on creating valuable, evergreen content that serves the audience consistently.

7. Failure to Measure and Adjust Strategies:

Misconception: Assuming that content strategies don't require constant evaluation and adjustment.

Reality: Regularly measuring performance metrics is crucial. Without analyzing data and adjusting strategies based on insights, it's challenging to improve content effectiveness.

8. Disregarding Content Promotion:

Misconception: Thinking that publishing content is the final step, neglecting the importance of content promotion.

Reality: Content promotion is as vital as content creation. Without effective distribution and promotion strategies, even exceptional content may go unnoticed.

9. Copying Competitors' Strategies Blindly:

Misconception: Assuming that replicating competitors' strategies directly will yield the same success.

Reality: Every business and audience is unique. While learning from competitors is valuable, blindly copying their strategies may not align with your specific audience or goals.

10. Failure to Adapt and Innovate:

Misconception: Believing that once a strategy is successful, it will always work without adapting to changes.

Reality: Markets, trends, and audience preferences evolve. Not adapting or innovating content strategies leads to stagnation and reduced competitiveness.

Understanding these misconceptions and ineffective strategies can help beginners steer clear of common pitfalls, allowing them to develop more effective and impactful content marketing initiatives.

ADVANCED CONTENT MARKETING STRATEGIES

Advanced content marketing strategies encompass more sophisticated approaches tailored for experienced marketers looking to further optimize their efforts and achieve higher-level goals. Here are some advanced strategies:

1. Personalization at Scale:

Dynamic Content: Utilize data-driven insights to create personalized content experiences for different audience segments.

AI and Automation: Implement AI-driven tools for content personalization, recommendation engines, and tailored messaging across various channels.

2. Interactive and Immersive Content:

Interactive Content: Develop engaging formats like quizzes, polls, calculators, and interactive infographics to enhance user engagement.

Immersive Experiences: Explore AR/VR technology to create immersive brand experiences and storytelling.

3. Account-Based Marketing (ABM):

Targeted Campaigns: Craft content specifically for high-value accounts or prospects to address their unique needs and pain points.

Personalized Touchpoints: Create tailored content experiences at different stages of the buyer's journey for individual accounts.

4. Content Atomization and Repurposing:

Content Atomization: Break down long-form content into smaller pieces (e.g., blog posts, infographics, social media snippets) for wider distribution.

Repurposing: Adapt content into different formats (e.g., turning blog posts into videos, podcasts, or webinars) to reach diverse audiences.

5. Thought Leadership and Original Research:

In-depth Research: Produce authoritative content through original research, surveys, or whitepapers, positioning your brand as an industry thought leader.

Long-Form, Insightful Content: Create comprehensive guides, case studies, or reports that offer unique insights and valuable data.

6. Content Localization and Global Expansion:

Localized Content: Tailor content for specific geographic regions, languages, or cultural nuances to expand the global audience.

International SEO: Implement SEO strategies considering regional search behaviors and keywords to enhance content discoverability in different markets.

7. Community Building and User-Generated Content (UGC):

Community Engagement: Foster communities around your brand through forums, social media groups, or dedicated platforms for discussions.

UGC Strategies: Encourage user-generated content like testimonials, reviews, or user stories to amplify brand credibility and engagement.

8. Omni-channel Content Distribution:

Multi-platform Approach: Develop content for various channels (website, social media, email, podcasts, webinars) to reach audiences across multiple touchpoints.

Consistent Messaging: Ensure consistent brand messaging and storytelling across all channels for a unified brand experience.

9. Data-Driven Optimization:

Predictive Analytics: Utilize predictive modeling and data analysis to forecast content performance and make proactive adjustments.

AI-powered Insights: Leverage AI algorithms to derive deep insights from data, guiding content strategies and personalization efforts.

10. Experimentation and Innovation:

Testing New Formats: Continuously experiment with emerging content formats, channels, and technologies to stay ahead of trends.

Iterative Improvement: Use data insights to iterate on content strategies, test hypotheses, and innovate continually.

Implementing these advanced strategies requires a deep understanding of your audience, robust data analysis, technological integration, and a willingness to experiment. By deploying these tactics strategically, experienced content marketers can elevate their campaigns, enhance engagement, and achieve more impactful results.

UPCOMING TRENDS AND HOW TO ADAPT TO CHANGES IN THE INDUSTRY.

Staying updated with upcoming trends in content marketing and adapting to industry changes are crucial for maintaining competitiveness and relevance. Here are some upcoming trends and strategies to adapt to these changes:

1. Video-first Approach:

Trend: Video content continues to dominate. Short-form videos (TikTok, Reels) and long-form video content (webinars, live streams) gain traction.

Adaptation: Invest in video content creation, leverage live video for engagement, and optimize for mobile consumption.

2. Voice Search Optimization:

Trend: The rise of voice-activated devices leads to increased voice searches, impacting SEO strategies.

Adaptation: Optimize content for voice search by using conversational language, answering specific questions, and focusing on long-tail keywords.

3. AI-driven Personalization:

Trend: AI-powered tools enable hyper-personalization and predictive content recommendations.

Adaptation: Implement AI-driven content personalization, leveraging data insights for tailored content experiences.

4. Interactive Content:

Trend: Interactive formats like polls, quizzes, AR/VR experiences, and shoppable content gain popularity for engaging audiences.

Adaptation: Experiment with interactive content to boost engagement and create immersive brand experiences.

5. Ephemeral Content and Stories:

Trend: Short-lived, temporary content on platforms like Instagram and Snapchat gains traction for authenticity.

Adaptation: Embrace ephemeral content for storytelling, behind-the-scenes glimpses, and real-time engagement with audiences.

6. Purpose-driven and Sustainable Content:

Trend: Consumers seek brands with a clear purpose and commitment to sustainability.

Adaptation: Integrate purpose-driven messaging and sustainability initiatives into content strategies to resonate with conscious consumers.

7. Content Localization and Global Expansion:

Trend: Brands increasingly focus on localized content strategies to cater to diverse global audiences.

Adaptation: Tailor content for specific regions, languages, and cultures to expand global reach and relevance.

8. Privacy and Data Protection:

Trend: Heightened concern for user privacy and data protection drives changes in data collection and usage.

Adaptation: Ensure compliance with privacy regulations (e.g., GDPR, CCPA), prioritize data security, and be transparent with users about data usage.

9. Community Engagement and UGC:

Trend: Building communities around brands and leveraging user-generated content enhances authenticity and trust.

Adaptation: Foster communities, encourage user participation, and leverage UGC to amplify brand advocacy and engagement.

10. AI-powered Content Creation and Automation:

Trend: AI-based tools assist in content creation, automation, and optimization processes.

Adaptation: Explore AI-driven content creation tools for generating personalized content, automating workflows, and improving efficiency.

Strategies for Adapting to Industry Changes:

• Continuous Learning: Stay updated with industry news, attend webinars, conferences, and courses to stay abreast of emerging trends and technologies.

• Experimentation and Testing: Allocate resources for testing new formats, channels, or tools to adapt and innovate within your content strategies.

• Data-driven Insights: Utilize analytics tools to gather data, analyze trends, and make informed decisions based on insights to optimize strategies.

• Agility and Flexibility: Stay agile in adapting strategies as per evolving market dynamics, technological advancements, and changing consumer behaviors.

• Collaboration and Networking: Engage with peers, network within the industry, and collaborate with experts to gain diverse perspectives and insights.

• Iterative Improvement: Continuously review and refine content strategies based on performance metrics and user feedback for iterative improvement.

Adapting to upcoming trends involves a proactive approach, embracing innovation, and a willingness to evolve strategies to meet evolving consumer demands and market shifts.

ETHICAL CONSIDERATIONS AND GUIDELINES IN CONTENT MARKETING

Ethical considerations in content marketing are fundamental to building trust, maintaining credibility, and fostering positive relationships with audiences. Here are key ethical guidelines:

1. Transparency and Authenticity:

Honesty: Be transparent about sponsorships, affiliations, or paid promotions within content.

Authenticity: Ensure content aligns with the brand's values and mission, avoiding deceptive practices.

2. Respect for Privacy and Data:

Data Handling: Collect and use consumer data responsibly, adhering to privacy laws and obtaining consent.

Data Security: Safeguard user information and maintain data confidentiality.

3. Accuracy and Truthfulness:

Factual Content: Ensure accuracy in information presented, fact-check claims, and cite credible sources.

Avoid Misleading Practices: Steer clear of false advertising, exaggerated claims, or misleading statements.

4. Fairness and Non-Discrimination:

Equal Representation: Embrace diversity and inclusivity in content representation without discrimination.

Avoid Stereotypes: Refrain from perpetuating stereotypes or biases in content creation.

5. User Experience and Safety:

User Safety: Prioritize user safety, especially in industries like health, finance, or advice-based content.

Avoid Harmful Content: Avoid content that incites violence, promotes hate speech, or encourages unethical behavior.

6. Content Legitimacy and Originality:

Plagiarism and Copyright: Respect intellectual property rights, give credit, and refrain from plagiarism.

Originality: Create original content and provide value rather than duplicating or repurposing without proper attribution.

7. Clear Communication and Consent:

Clear Disclosures: Clearly disclose sponsored content, affiliate links, or paid promotions.

User Consent: Obtain user consent for data collection, subscriptions, or any interactions requiring user input.

8. Responsibility in Advertising:

Compliance with Advertising Standards: Adhere to advertising regulations and guidelines set by relevant authorities.

Avoid Deceptive Advertising: Ensure advertisements are not misleading or deceptive.

9. Community Engagement and Responsiveness:

Engage Responsibly: Engage with audiences respectfully, address feedback, and handle criticism ethically.

Accountability: Take responsibility for mistakes, rectify errors promptly, and apologize when necessary.

10. Continuous Education and Improvement:

Stay Informed: Keep abreast of evolving ethical standards, industry best practices, and legal regulations.

Feedback and Adaptation: Listen to audience feedback, adapt to changes, and continually improve ethical standards.

By adhering to these ethical guidelines, content marketers can build credibility, foster trust with their audience, and contribute to a more transparent and responsible digital marketing landscape.

TIPS FOR STAYING UPDATED WITH CHANGES IN ALGORITHMS AND PLATFORMS

Staying updated with changes in algorithms and platforms is crucial for effective content marketing. Here are some tips to keep abreast of these updates:

1. Follow Official Sources:

Official Blogs and Documentation: Regularly check official blogs, documentation, and forums of platforms like Google, Facebook, Twitter, etc. for announcements and updates.

2. Subscribe to Industry News and Blogs:

Marketing Publications: Subscribe to marketing-focused websites, blogs, and newsletters (e.g., Moz, Search Engine Journal, HubSpot) for insights into algorithm changes and industry updates.

Social Media News: Follow influential marketers, industry experts, and official social media accounts for real-time updates.

3. Attend Webinars and Conferences:

Industry Events: Participate in webinars, virtual summits, and industry conferences where experts discuss the latest trends, updates, and best practices.

4. Join Online Communities:

Forums and Groups: Engage in industry-specific forums, groups (e.g., Reddit communities, LinkedIn groups), and social media discussions where professionals share insights and updates.

5. Utilize RSS Feeds and Aggregators:

RSS Readers: Use RSS feed readers to aggregate content from various industry-specific websites and blogs in one place for easy access.

Content Aggregators: Platforms like Feedly can help organize and curate content from different sources.

6. Monitor Analytics and Performance:

Analytics Tools: Regularly monitor analytics platforms (Google Analytics, social media analytics) to detect shifts in traffic, engagement, or user behavior that might correlate with algorithm changes.

7. Engage in Continuous Learning:

Online Courses and Certifications: Enroll in courses or certifications related to digital marketing and SEO to stay updated with the latest practices.

E-learning Platforms: Platforms like Coursera, Udemy, and LinkedIn Learning offer courses on SEO, digital marketing, and algorithm updates.

8. Network and Collaborate:

Networking Events: Attend local or virtual meetups, workshops, and networking events to connect with peers and learn about their experiences and insights.

9. Set Up Google Alerts:

Customized Alerts: Use Google Alerts to receive notifications about specific keywords or phrases related to algorithm updates, industry news, or platform changes.

10. Experiment and Test:

A/B Testing: Conduct A/B tests on your content, SEO strategies, or advertising campaigns to observe changes in performance, which could indicate platform or algorithm updates.

11. Follow Platform Documentation and Guidelines:

Adhere to Guidelines: Regularly review and adhere to the guidelines provided by platforms to ensure compliance and stay updated with policy changes.

12. Engage with Experts and Ask Questions:

Q&A Platforms: Utilize platforms like Quora or Reddit to ask questions and engage with experts or professionals in the field.

By employing these strategies, content marketers can stay informed about changes in algorithms, social media platforms, search engines, and other digital marketing channels, enabling them to adapt their strategies effectively and maintain a competitive edge in the evolving digital landscape.

THE INDUSTRY BEST PRACTICES

Here are some industry best practices in the field of content marketing:

• Quality Over Quantity: Prioritize creating high-quality, valuable content that resonates with your audience rather than focusing solely on quantity.

• Audience-Centric Approach: Understand your audience's needs, preferences, and pain points to create content that addresses their specific challenges and interests.

• Consistent Brand Voice: Maintain a consistent brand voice and messaging across all content to reinforce brand identity and build recognition.

• Multichannel Distribution: Leverage various channels (website, social media, email, podcasts, video, etc.) to reach audiences across diverse platforms and touchpoints.

• Data-Driven Strategies: Utilize analytics tools to gather insights, measure performance metrics, and make informed decisions for optimizing content strategies.

• SEO Integration: Incorporate SEO best practices, keyword optimization, and mobile-friendly content to improve search engine visibility and rankings.

• Engagement and Interaction: Encourage audience engagement through interactive content, user-generated content, and fostering community participation.

• Storytelling and Authenticity: Craft compelling narratives that resonate emotionally with your audience, emphasizing authenticity and genuine storytelling.

• Continuous Improvement: Regularly review and refine content strategies based on performance metrics, audience feedback, and industry trends for ongoing improvement.

EXAMPLES ILLUSTRATING SUCCESSFUL CONTENT MARKETING CAMPAIGNS.

Here are some examples of successful content marketing campaigns that have made a significant impact:

Red Bull: Stratos Jump

• Campaign: Red Bull Stratos Jump

• Objective: Red Bull sponsored Felix Baumgartner's record-breaking freefall from the stratosphere. It aimed to showcase extreme sports and push the limits of human achievement.

• Content Strategy: The entire event was live-streamed online, accompanied by engaging content, behind-the-scenes footage, documentaries, and interviews, creating anticipation and excitement.

• Impact: Red Bull's content strategy around the event generated massive online viewership, social media buzz, and media coverage, effectively showcasing the brand's association with high-energy, extreme activities.

Airbnb: #LiveThere Campaign

• Campaign: #LiveThere Campaign by Airbnb

• Objective: Shift the focus from traditional tourist spots to the authentic local experience offered by Airbnb rentals.

• Content Strategy: Created a series of city-specific travel guides, videos, and social media campaigns emphasizing local neighborhoods, culture, and unique experiences.

• Impact: The campaign resonated with travelers seeking authentic experiences, significantly increasing user engagement and bookings. It helped position Airbnb as a platform offering more than just accommodations.

Dove: Real Beauty Campaign

• Campaign: Dove Real Beauty Campaign

• Objective: Challenge beauty stereotypes and promote self-esteem among women by celebrating diverse body types and natural beauty.

• Content Strategy: Released a series of videos, print ads, and social media content showcasing real women of different sizes, shapes, and backgrounds, encouraging self-acceptance and confidence.

• Impact: The campaign garnered widespread attention, praise, and discussion around societal beauty standards. It resonated with audiences, leading to increased brand loyalty and positive brand perception.

Nike: Just Do It

• Campaign: Nike's Just Do It Campaign

• Objective: Inspire athletes and individuals to overcome obstacles and pursue their goals and dreams.

• Content Strategy: Created powerful and motivational ads featuring athletes sharing their stories of determination and resilience, accompanied by the iconic "Just Do It" slogan.

• Impact: The campaign became a timeless and iconic representation of Nike's brand ethos, resonating with audiences worldwide and contributing to Nike's brand loyalty and market dominance.

Blendtec: Will It Blend?

• Campaign: Blendtec's "Will It Blend?" Series

• Objective: Showcase the power and durability of Blendtec blenders by blending unusual and unconventional items.

• Content Strategy: Created a YouTube video series where the company's founder blended items like iPhones, golf balls, and even a crowbar, demonstrating the blender's strength in an entertaining way.

• Impact: The viral video series boosted brand awareness, increased product sales, and demonstrated the blender's quality and reliability in a fun and memorable manner.

GoPro: User-Centric Content and Community Engagement

• Strategy: GoPro encourages its users to share their action-packed videos and photos taken using GoPro cameras. They curate user-generated content on their social media platforms, website, and YouTube channel, celebrating their community of adventurous users.

• Success: GoPro's strategy leverages user-generated content to showcase the capabilities of their cameras. By highlighting the experiences of their users, they've built a passionate community, resulting in increased brand loyalty and sales.

HubSpot: Educational and Inbound Marketing

• Strategy: HubSpot focuses on inbound marketing by providing valuable educational content through blogs, e-books, webinars, and free tools. They offer a wealth of information on marketing, sales, and customer service, positioning themselves as industry thought leaders.

• Success: By consistently providing educational content, HubSpot has built a vast audience of marketers and business professionals seeking valuable insights. This strategy has positioned them as a trusted authority in the marketing software industry.

These successful content marketing campaigns showcase creativity, authenticity, relevance, and storytelling, aligning with audience interests and needs to create lasting impressions and drive engagement and sales.

WHAT MADE THESE CAMPAIGNS SUCCESSFUL AND HOW BEGINNERS CAN APPLY SIMILAR TACTICS

Here's an analysis of the key elements that contributed to the success of these campaigns and how beginners can adapt these tactics:

1. Compelling Storytelling and Emotion:

What made it successful: Engaging storytelling evokes emotions, capturing audience attention and fostering a connection.

How beginners can apply it: Craft compelling narratives that resonate emotionally with your audience. Share stories that evoke emotions, entertain, or educate while aligning with your brand's values and goals.

2. User-Generated Content (UGC) and Community Engagement:

What made it successful: Leveraging UGC builds authenticity, fosters community, and encourages user participation.

How beginners can apply it: Encourage your audience to create content related to your brand. Build communities, engage with users, and showcase their experiences to create a sense of belonging.

3. Entertaining and Educational Content:

What made it successful: Entertaining and educational content captures attention and provides value to the audience.

How beginners can apply it: Create content that educates, entertains, or solves problems for your audience. Utilize humor, creativity, or valuable information to engage and resonate with them.

4. Viral and Shareable Content:

What made it successful: Viral content has shareable qualities, often combining humor, uniqueness, or surprise elements.

How beginners can apply it: Strive to create content that is shareable and has the potential to go viral by incorporating elements that resonate deeply with your audience and encourage sharing.

5. Consistency and Brand Authenticity:

What made it successful: Consistent content delivery and maintaining brand authenticity build trust and recognition.

How beginners can apply it: Establish a consistent content schedule and maintain a coherent brand voice across all platforms. Be authentic, transparent, and genuine in your communications.

6. Audience-Centric Approach:

What made it successful: Understanding audience needs and preferences drives content relevance and engagement.

How beginners can apply it: Conduct thorough audience research to comprehend your target audience. Tailor content to address their specific challenges, desires, or interests.

7. Value Proposition and Clear Messaging:

What made it successful: Clear and concise messaging that communicates the brand's value proposition effectively.

How beginners can apply it: Clearly articulate your brand's value proposition in your content. Highlight how your product or service solves problems or fulfills needs for your audience.

8. Use of Multiple Content Formats and Channels:

What made it successful: Leveraging various content formats and channels increases reach and engages diverse audiences.

How beginners can apply it: Experiment with different content formats (videos, blogs, infographics) and distribution channels (social media, email, website) to reach a broader audience.

9. Innovation and Experimentation:

What made it successful: Embracing innovation and experimenting with new ideas lead to fresh, engaging content.

How beginners can apply it: Be open to trying new content ideas, formats, or channels. Test, measure, and learn from the outcomes to refine your strategies.

10. Measurable Goals and Analysis:

What made it successful: Setting measurable goals and analyzing performance helps track success and make data-driven decisions.

How beginners can apply it: Define clear goals for your content marketing efforts and use analytics tools to track key performance metrics. Analyze the results and adjust strategies accordingly.

By incorporating these tactics into their content marketing strategies, beginners can create engaging, valuable content that resonates with their audience, fosters engagement, and drives success in the digital landscape.

CONCLUSION

In conclusion, content marketing stands as an indispensable cornerstone in today's digital era, serving as the bridge that connects businesses with their audiences in a meaningful and impactful way. As discussed, content marketing transcends mere promotional tactics; it embodies a strategic approach rooted in delivering value, building trust, and fostering lasting relationships with consumers.

At its core, content marketing revolves around understanding and addressing the needs, preferences, and pain points of the target audience. By employing an audience-centric strategy, content marketers can create compelling, high-quality content that resonates authentically with their viewers, irrespective of the platform or format.

The evolution of content marketing brings forth various best practices and trends crucial for success. From embracing video as a dominant medium to personalizing content at scale and optimizing for voice search, staying updated and adapting to these trends is paramount. Moreover, ethical considerations, such as transparency, authenticity, and respect for user data, serve as guiding principles that underpin every content marketing endeavor.

The journey through content marketing encompasses a structured approach – from meticulous planning and goal setting to comprehensive audience research, content creation, distribution, and continuous analysis. Alongside this, the iterative process of improvement, experimentation, and learning forms the backbone for refining strategies and achieving sustainable growth.

In essence, content marketing transcends the realm of marketing—it embodies storytelling, innovation, and a commitment to delivering value. By adhering to ethical guidelines, leveraging current trends, and adopting best practices, content marketers can forge stronger connections, drive engagement, and pave the way for long-term success in the dynamic and ever-evolving digital landscape. As the landscape continues to evolve, content marketers equipped with adaptability, creativity, and a dedication to consumer-centricity will navigate these changes to create compelling narratives that resonate and endure.

www.ingramcontent.com/pod-product-compliance
Lightning Source LLC
Chambersburg PA
CBHW072200290526
45794CB00004B/1590